AF086638

What's that bird?

What's that bird?

Rob Hume

THIS EDITION

DK LONDON
Editor Annie Moss
Managing Editor Angeles Gavira
Senior Art Editor Ina Stradins
Managing Art Editor Michael Duffy
Senior Production Controller Meskerem Berhane
Art Director Maxine Pedliham
Publishing Director Georgina Dee

DK DELHI
Editors Saumya Agarwal, Aashline R. Avarachan
Senior Managing Editor Rohan Sinha
Senior Art Editors Mahua Mandal, Pooja Pipil
Managing Art Editor Sudakshina Basu
Project Jacket Designer Tanya Mehrotra
Senior Jackets Coordinator Priyanka Sharma Saddi
Senior DTP Designer Harish Aggarwal
Pre-Production Designer Raman Panwar
Pre-Production Coordinator Tarun Sharma
Pre-Production Manager Balwant Singh
Creative Head Malavika Talukder

FIRST EDITION

DK LONDON
Senior Art Editor Jacqui Swan
Senior Editor Angeles Gavira
Editor Lizzie Munsey
Production Editor Tony Phipps
Production Controller Emma Sparks
Jacket Designer Laura Brim
Picture Researcher Evi Peroulaki
CTS Adam Brackenbury
Managing Art Editor Michelle Baxter
Managing Editor Camilla Hallinan
Publisher Sarah Larter
Art Director Philip Ormerod
Associate Publishing Director Liz Wheeler
Publishing Director Jonathan Metcalf

DK DELHI
Deputy Managing Art Editor Mitun Banerjee
Managing Editor Rohan Sinha
Deputy Managing Editor Alka Thakur Hazarika
Senior Art Editor Ivy Roy
Designers Arijit Ganguly, Arup Giri, Pooja Pawwar, Khundongdam Rakesh
Editors Megha Gupta, Priyanka Nath
DTP Designer Bimlesh Tiwary
DTP Manager/CTS Balwant Singh
Production Manager Pankaj Sharma

This edition published in 2026
First published in Great Britain in 2012 by
Dorling Kindersley Limited
20 Vauxhall Bridge Road,
London SW1V 2SA

The authorised representative in the EEA is
Dorling Kindersley Verlag GmbH. Arnulfstr. 124,
80636 Munich, Germany

Copyright © 2012, 2026
Dorling Kindersley Limited
A Penguin Random House Company
10 9 8 7 6 5 4 3 2 1
001–345127–Jan/2026

All rights reserved. No part of this publication
may be reproduced, stored in or introduced into
a retrieval system, or transmitted, in any form, or by
any means (electronic, mechanical, photocopying,
recording, or otherwise), without the prior written
permission of the copyright owner.
No part of this publication may be used
or reproduced in any manner for the purpose
of training artificial intelligence technologies or
systems. In accordance with Article 4(3) of the DSM
Directive 2019/790, DK expressly reserves this work
from the text and data mining exception.

A CIP catalogue record for this book
is available from the British Library.
ISBN: 978-0-2417-1916-9

Printed and bound in China

www.dk.com

ABOUT THE AUTHOR

As a writer, editor, and identification expert, **Rob Hume** is much in demand for his expertise on birds. A lifelong birdwatcher, he worked for the Royal Society for the Protection of Birds (RSPB) for 35 years, and edited the RSPB's award-winning *Birds* magazine, which has a readership of 1.8 million, for 20 years. For several years he was on the editorial board of the influential *British Birds* magazine and chaired the British Birds Rarities Committee. Rob continues to be an active editor, for the RSPB and others.

MIX
Paper | Supporting
responsible forestry
FSC™ C018179

This book was made with Forest Stewardship Council™ certified paper – one small step in DK's commitment to a sustainable future.

Learn more at www.dk.com/uk/information/sustainability

Contents

Introduction **6**
Identifying Birds **8**

BIRD PROFILES **15**

1 CLOSE TO HOME **16**

2 WOODLAND & FOREST **32**

3 OPEN COUNTRY **42**

4 WATER & WATERSIDE **60**

5 COAST & SEA **90**

BIRD GALLERY **103**

Scientific Names **122**
Glossary **125**
Index **126**
Acknowledgments **128**

Introduction

Birds are fantastic creatures. They are unique not because they fly, or lay eggs, but because no other animal group has feathers. This book will help you identify the birds you see close to home and in easy-to-reach places. It provides simple profiles for the most common birds, with straightforward language and clear photos to highlight the key differences between similar-looking species. Each species is marked by distinctive shapes and colours, calls and songs. Some have different colours according to age, sex, and season. This book cannot cover all variations, but it gives you a good start. Living life at a fast pace, birds enjoy relatively brief, energetic lives, although some, such as Fulmars (40 years) and swans (25), live longer. The world's greatest globetrotters, millions of birds such as geese and terns migrate thousands of kilometres twice every year. Easier to see and more abundant than mammals, birds are the most accessible wild creatures. There are no rules about watching birds; you just need enthusiasm, an enquiring mind, a pair of binoculars, and a notebook. So look around you and enjoy the birds!

Rob Hume

Identifying Birds

Learning to tell which bird is which needs time and practice, but that is all part of the fun. Identifying birds also requires discipline: don't leap to conclusions but look carefully for the features that prove your identification, such as colour, size, shape, specific patterns, or particular calls.

Size

This is hard to judge: two birds of the same length can appear to be different sizes if they are not the same shape. The size of very similar-looking birds may surprise you: a Great Black-backed Gull is not much longer than a Lesser Black-backed Gull, but side by side it seems "twice as big" – and it is twice the weight. For the waders shown here, size is the main distinguishing feature.

DUNLIN

BAR-TAILED GODWIT

REDSHANK

CURLEW

SIZE, SHAPE, COLOUR, & MARKINGS

PIGEON — Heavy body, Small head
RED GROUSE — Thickset body
WREN — Tiny tail
SWALLOW — Slender shape
RED-BREASTED MERGANSER — Long body

Shape
Even experts can struggle to describe bird shapes: a "slim" bird might actually be quite "rounded" but with a long neck or tail, or look slim from the side but broader end-on. The best way to learn to identify birds by shape is to learn some shapes and then relate what you see to familiar birds.

BLUE TIT — Eye-stripe, Cap
CHAFFINCH — Wing pattern
DUNNOCK — Streaks
MISTLE THRUSH — Spots
RED-LEGGED PARTRIDGE — Eye-ring, Bars

Colour and markings
The traditional "field marks" of birds include eye-stripes, wingbars, streaks, spots, and white tail sides. These can help your identification but require good, clear views of the bird. You will use field marks all the time at first, but later rely on other factors: for example, you will soon be identifying Robins and Blue Tits in silhouette without seeing any colour at all! It all comes down to experience: you learn more year by year and enjoy birds more the longer you watch them.

Flight

Most small birds are difficult to identify in flight, as they dash past and dive into cover. Larger species provide more useful clues, and many big birds, such as birds of prey, spend long spells in the air. Some birds are quite easy to see in the air but are rarely (such as the Hobby) or never (Swift) seen on the ground.

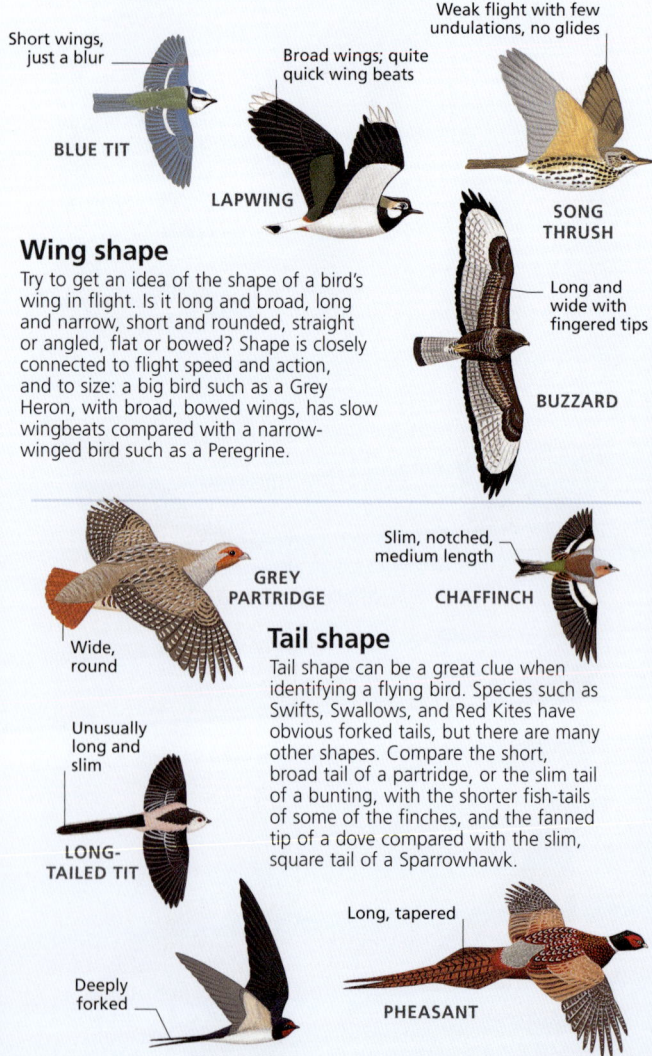

Short wings, just a blur — **BLUE TIT**

Broad wings; quite quick wing beats — **LAPWING**

Weak flight with few undulations, no glides — **SONG THRUSH**

Long and wide with fingered tips — **BUZZARD**

Wing shape

Try to get an idea of the shape of a bird's wing in flight. Is it long and broad, long and narrow, short and rounded, straight or angled, flat or bowed? Shape is closely connected to flight speed and action, and to size: a big bird such as a Grey Heron, with broad, bowed wings, has slow wingbeats compared with a narrow-winged bird such as a Peregrine.

GREY PARTRIDGE — Wide, round

CHAFFINCH — Slim, notched, medium length

LONG-TAILED TIT — Unusually long and slim

SWALLOW — Deeply forked

PHEASANT — Long, tapered

Tail shape

Tail shape can be a great clue when identifying a flying bird. Species such as Swifts, Swallows, and Red Kites have obvious forked tails, but there are many other shapes. Compare the short, broad tail of a partridge, or the slim tail of a bunting, with the shorter fish-tails of some of the finches, and the fanned tip of a dove compared with the slim, square tail of a Sparrowhawk.

Flight pattern

Size, shape, and flight action are closely linked, but some small, aerial birds (such as the Swift) glide and swoop like larger species, and some big, round-winged birds (like the Pheasant) have very fast beats. Try to describe what you see: fast, whirring flaps and undulations; slow flaps and floating glides; relaxed, "elastic" flaps compared with stiff, jerky beats, and so on. These diagrams show some of the different flight patterns you might come across.

wingbeats

Finch-like: sequence of short, fast bursts of beats between undulating glides

Woodpecker-like: bursts of beats between deep swoops with wings closed

Swallow-like: sideslips and swoops with fluid, relaxed wingbeats; bursts of wingbeats between glides

Duck-like: consistent, fast, deep wingbeats, without glides except when descending to land or water

Sound

Most birds are extremely vocal: they call to keep in touch. Some call loudly in flight, and many have loud, persistent songs with sounds and patterns characteristic of their species. You hear more birds than you see (and find most by hearing them first), so learning their sounds is invaluable as well as great fun. Many birds look so similar that listening to them is the best way to tell them apart.

GREENSHANK
Even, ringing *tew-tew-tew*

GOLDFINCH
Lisping, tinkling *skip-i-lip*

REDSHANK
"Bouncing", descending *tyew-yu-yu, teu, teu-hu*

Season

Not all birds can be seen everywhere all year round. Some, such as Swallows and Cuckoos, are strictly "summer visitors" to the UK, arriving in spring and leaving in autumn. Others, such as Fieldfares and Bewick's Swans, arrive in autumn and spend the winter in the UK. Still others are seen only in passing on their migration in spring or autumn.

Wagtails

In winter, a wagtail with yellow under the tail will always be a Grey Wagtail, as the Yellow Wagtail is only present from April to October. No Yellow Wagtails spend the winter in northern Europe.

GREY WAGTAIL

YELLOW WAGTAIL

Pipits

The Meadow Pipit looks very similar to the Tree Pipit, but identification problems can be forgotten between October and March, when the Tree Pipit is in Africa.

TREE PIPIT

MEADOW PIPIT

Behaviour

It is easy to see differences in bird behaviour, even in the garden: look at the perky cockiness of a tail-flicking, head-bobbing, bold Robin compared with the quiet, shy shuffle of a Dunnock. Wherever you are, there will be birds with distinctive characteristics that are always worth learning. Use your own words to describe them: you will remember them more easily.

Dunnock
Sits upright to sing, but shuffles low and horizontally to feed, with little outward flicks of its tail feathers.

Great Tit
Quite "heavy" for a small bird; crashes about more than a Blue Tit and feeds on or near the ground more often.

Grey Heron
A waterside bird, but nests in treetops, and stands around in small groups for hours in dry fields.

House Sparrow
Sits on an obvious perch, flicking its tail, and cheeps. Also gathers in noisy, squabbling groups that bash about in hedges and thickets.

Treecreeper
Treecreepers are unable to stand or walk properly. They are strictly creepers on tree bark.

Parts of a Bird

Feathers are neatly arranged in particular groups, called tracts. In any species, the position, size, shape, and number of feathers in each tract are remarkably consistent.

Naming the parts

Using simple terms and names for the tracts, we can write a detailed description of any bird. Here, a Starling is shown perched and in flight, to show where the same feathers are in both positions. The labels on these Starlings show all you need to know to begin with. Some terms are further explained in the Glossary (p.125).

BIRD PROFILES

Starting close to home and then looking a little farther afield, these are the most common birds you can expect to see, grouped by habitat and then by appearance. Some birds can be seen in more than one habitat, but are dealt with here in the most likely one. Where males and females look significantly different, or both sexes are shown, a symbol is shown.

16 CLOSE TO HOME
32 WOODLAND AND FOREST
42 OPEN COUNTRY
60 WATER AND WATERSIDE
90 COAST AND SEA

Symbols
♀ Female
♂ Male
↔ Length

WREN
P.19

BLACKBIRD
Male, p.24

ROBIN
P.19

Garden

Flowers, shrubs, lawns, trees, and earth can make gardens a miniature mixture of other habitats. Some birds thrive in this patchwork, and more can be encouraged in by food, water, and the shelter provided by shrubs and trees.

1 CLOSE TO HOME

Habitats on your doorstep are often rich and varied: don't neglect the possibilities of gardens, town parks and ponds, and the nearest country park. You can often learn to identify common birds here before venturing further afield.

MALLARD
Male, p.62

MOORHEN
P.73

Pond or park lake

Wild ducks and waterbirds such as Mallards, Mute Swans, Moorhens, and several kinds of gulls easily take to suburban or even urban lakes – you never quite know what might turn up next.

House

If you are lucky, you may have birds on or around the house: House Sparrows, Starlings, and Swifts can be seen around homes, and House Martins even nest under the eaves of buildings.

HOUSE MARTIN
P.30

HOUSE SPARROW
P.18

Town centre

Even a city centre can offer a chance to see at least a few birds: Town Pigeons and maybe a Kestrel or a Peregrine overhead. There is also the chance of a Swift or two, and probably a Pied Wagtail.

TOWN PIGEON
P.28

KESTREL
P.54

Small Brown Birds

These small birds are seen around homes, offices, and gardens. You can tell them apart by looking at their shapes and movement.

DUNNOCK

Streaky brown and grey; darker than Robin, thinner beak than sparrow. Creeping, shuffly gait. Sits upright when singing its fast, warbling song.
↔ 14cm

- Thin beak
- Grey neck
- Streaked back
- Streaked sides

HOUSE SPARROW ♂

Cheeky, chirruping, lively, and bold; a sociable bird of thickets, hedges, and buildings. Female is paler than male, with no black bib.
↔ 14cm

- White bar on wing
- Grey cap
- Thick, triangular beak
- Black bib
- Plain underneath

HOUSE SPARROW ♀

Sociable, groups give lively chirruping, chattering chorus. Often feeds on open ground but rests inside bushes or flies up to roofs.
↔ 14cm

- Broad buff band behind eye
- Thick yellow-brown beak
- Streaks of yellow-buff and brown
- Underside unstreaked buff

SMALL BROWN BIRDS

What to look out for • Beak shape • Streaked or plain back • Face and cheek pattern • Hop, walk, or shuffle • Flicks of wings and tail

TREE SPARROW

Similar to male House Sparrow but rare in gardens; found on farmland with old trees. Brown cap with no grey centre.
↔ 14cm

Black ear-spot · Brown cap · Black chin · Plain underside

ROBIN

Small and cocky, with hop-hop-stop-and-look action. No red on young birds. Often sings loud, warbling song under lights at night.
↔ 14cm

Plain brown back · Flicks tail and wings · Bold, dark eye · Pale, orange-red breast

WREN

Tiny, feisty, barred brown bird of low, dense vegetation. Its short tail is often cocked up. Loud, trilling and warbling song.

Barred, reddish brown back and wings · Pale stripe over eye · Short, thin, stiff tail · Rusty orange sides

↔ 9–10cm

Finches

These sparrow-like finches have thick beaks and forked tails. Their beak shapes vary depending on what they eat. Some use feeders; others eat food spilled from them.

GOLDFINCH

Slender and sharp-beaked, with striking face pattern and yellow-banded wings. Found in small groups on thistles and other weeds.

↔ 12.5–13cm

- White cheek and neck
- Dark red face
- Yellow across black wing
- Forked tail, visible in flight

GREENFINCH

Stocky, unstreaked, and big-beaked, with yellow wing and tail flashes. Often found on feeders. Sings loud trills from treetops.

↔ 15cm

- Thick, pale beak
- Dark eye-patch
- Yellow edge to wing
- Unstreaked, dull green underside

SISKIN ♂

Much smaller than Greenfinch, with black cap and bars on wings. Often found on birdfeeders or in tall trees with seeds and cones.

↔ 12cm

- Black cap
- Streaked green back
- Yellow on neck and breast
- Yellow flashes on tail and wing

FINCHES

What to look out for • Beak size and shape • Streaked or unstreaked above and below • Shape and colour of bars on wings • Rump and tail patches

CHAFFINCH ♂

Sparrow-sized and unstreaked, with slim, notched tail and bold, white wing marks. Male pinkest in spring, dull-headed in winter. Female drab but same pattern. Bright, rattling song.
↔ 14.5cm

- Blue cap
- White shoulder patch
- White bar on wing
- Unmarked, pale pink underside

BULLFINCH ♂

Stocky, upright, and colourful, with square white patch on rump; female is duller but same pattern as male. Secretive but makes loud, flat, simple whistle.
↔ 15cm

- Black cap and chin
- Unstreaked, pink-red breast
- Grey bar on wing
- White patch below and above tail

BRAMBLING ♂

Shape like Chaffinch but has orange wing and breast patch with a white belly. Blacker head and beak in summer. Often found under beech trees.
↔ 14.5cm

- Black and orange bars on wing
- Yellow beak in winter
- Orange shoulder patch
- White rump, visible in flight

Thrushes

These ground- or berry-feeding birds hop around on the grass, flying up to trees if disturbed. They may gather in groups outside the breeding season.

What to look out for • Streaks, stripes, or spots beneath • Head pattern • Plain or pale-streaked wings • Rump/tail contrast

SONG THRUSH

Small, speckled thrush of woods, lawns, and gardens. Plain back, wings, and tail. Song repeats each phrase several times.
↔ 23cm

- Faint head pattern
- Brown wing feathers
- V-shaped spots on chest and sides
- Plain brown tail

MISTLE THRUSH

Big, bold, upright thrush that makes long, leaping hops on ground. Loud, repetitive song and dry, chattering call.
↔ 27cm

- Pale edges to wing feathers
- Pale eye-ring
- Bold spots on chest and sides
- White edge to tail

THRUSHES 23

REDWING

Small, dark, sociable thrush. Often gathers in flocks in fields, scarcer in gardens. Thin *seep* call.
↔ 21cm

- Broad, pale stripe over eye
- Pale stripe under cheek
- Reddish patch under wing
- Streaked underneath

FIELDFARE

A large, striking thrush with grey on its head and rump. Often gathers in wandering flocks. Chuckling *chak-chak* calls.
↔ 25cm

- Grey patch above black tail
- Yellow beak
- Black around eye
- Black spots on chest and sides

BLACKBIRD ♀

Familiar garden and woodland thrush. Female is brown with subtle, dark spots beneath. Runs, hops, and feeds on ground and in bushes. Juvenile is more rufous with black bill.
↔ 24–25cm

- Dark, smoky brown tail, back, and rump
- Yellow or blackish beak
- Throat spotted or streaked
- Underside much darker than Song Thrush

♂ p.24

Medium-sized Garden Birds

These birds include a black thrush and a blackish starling, both likely to feed on lawns; a rare and exciting garden visitor; and a bold, opportunistic, piebald crow.

BLACKBIRD ♂

Familiar garden and woodland thrush. Often raises tail slowly after a short run. Pulls worms out of lawns. Loud, musical song; *pink pink!* alarm and *chook* calls.

↔ 24–25cm

Yellow eye-ring
Yellow beak
Black plumage
Wide, longish tail

♀ p.23

STARLING

Spotted in winter, shiny in summer; juvenile drab brown. This is a short-tailed, busy bird. Walks on the ground and has fast, sharp-winged flight. Rattles and whistles in song. Huge flocks look like smoke clouds from a distance.

↔ 21cm

Sharp, yellow beak
Glossy black body with green and purple sheen
Long, strong, red-brown legs
Short, square tail, kept down

MEDIUM-SIZED GARDEN BIRDS | 25

What to look out for • Tail length and shape • Spotted or unspotted plumage • Crest or no crest • Feeding actions

WAXWING

Starling-like shape but dumpier. Unique crest on head. Often very tame. Visits in winter, stripping trees of berries. Flocks rest in trees between bouts of feeding. Call a high trill.

↔ 18cm

Upright, pointed crest

Yellow, red, and white on wing

Black bib

Yellow tail tip

MAGPIE

Big, black-and-white bird, with long tail. Often gathers in groups that make loud, clattering calls. Builds big, untidy nests that are obvious in winter when leaves fall.

↔ 44–46cm

Black head and chest

Big, white shoulder patch

Long, glossy, green-purple tail

White underneath

Blue Tit & Relatives

These tiny, acrobatic, and boldly marked birds often come to feeding stations and bird tables, but are equally at home in woods and hedgerows.

What to look out for • Yellow, green, or blue colour on body • Head pattern • Underside colour, especially on chin or throat • Tail shape

GREAT TIT

A small, agile bird with striking head pattern. Common in gardens and woodlands; often seen on feeders. Strident, two-note *tee-cher* song.

↔ 14cm

- Black head
- White cheek
- Black, central stripe on breast
- Green back
- White sides to tail

BLUE TIT

Greenish or yellowish bird with white face. Blue cap, wings, and tail seen at closer range. Fairly tame and noisy; often found on feeders.

↔ 11.5cm

- Blue cap
- Dark stripe on white face
- Pale yellow underside
- Grey-blue tail

BLUE TIT & RELATIVES

COAL TIT

Grey-brown tit with no yellow, green, or blue on body, unlike Great or Blue tits; striking head pattern. Carries nuts away from feeders to eat nearby.
↔ 11.5cm

LONG-TAILED TIT

Tiny-beaked bird with plump, round body and long, thin tail. Small flocks fly in single files between bushes. Low purr and sharp, whistled calls.
↔ 14cm

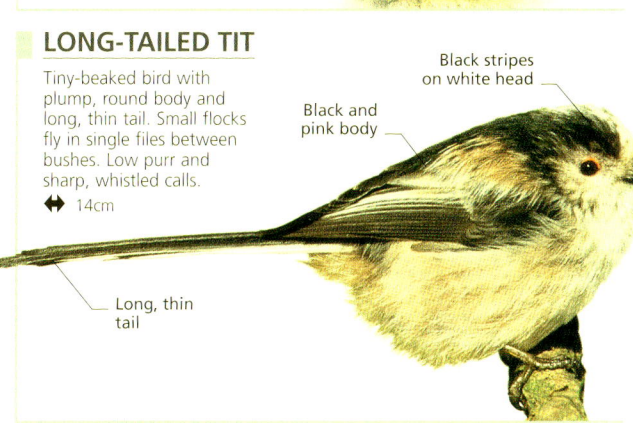

MARSH TIT

Plain brown, buff, and black tit with no green, yellow, or blue on body. Often seen in woods and bushes; scarce on feeders. Loud *pit-chew!* call.
↔ 11.5cm

Pigeons & Doves

These are medium to large birds with soft plumage, rounded heads, and short legs and beaks. They are at home in trees and bushes or on the ground.

What to look out for • Head and neck pattern • Wing patterns • Tail patterns above and below • Size (Woodpigeon the biggest)

TOWN PIGEON

Familiar town-square bird, the "racing pigeon" gone wild. Varies in colour. Descended from Rock Dove, which still occurs in parts of northwest Europe, nesting on cliffs.

↔ 31–35cm

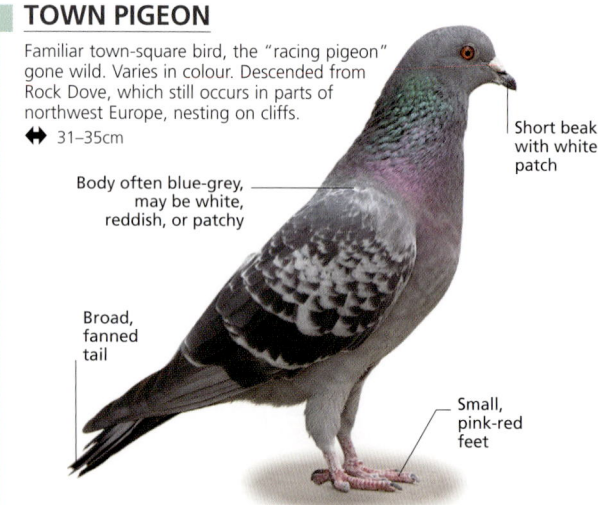

- Short beak with white patch
- Body often blue-grey, may be white, reddish, or patchy
- Broad, fanned tail
- Small, pink-red feet

WOODPIGEON

The biggest pigeon, with the longest wings and tail. Clatters loudly when taking flight. Sings soft *coo-coooo-coo-cu-cooo* song.

↔ 40–42cm

- Big, white patch on neck of adult
- Pink chest
- White patch on wing
- Black and pale grey bands on tail
- White on wing

STOCK DOVE

A small woodland or parkland pigeon with no white on wings or neck. Not a town bird, often found on fields with Woodpigeons.

✥ 32–34cm

- Round, blue-grey head
- Dark-edged wings with pale grey centre
- No white on wing
- Two short, dark bars on wing

COLLARED DOVE

A common dove, seen year-round; a garden bird. Slender, long-tailed, and very pale in colour. Sings three-note *cu-cooo-cuk* song; nasal *whurrr* call in flight.

✥ 31–33cm

- Black collar
- Pinkish, sandy grey wings and body
- Slim, elongated shape
- Tail black beneath with white tip

TURTLE DOVE

The smallest, most delicate dove; seen from April to September. Found in woods, hedges, and thickets; not a garden bird. Makes long, purring *coo*.

✥ 26–28cm

- Striped neck patch
- Chequered back
- Pink breast
- Black tail with white tip

Birds of Summer Skies

These are aerial feeders that catch insects over fields (Swallow), houses (House Martin), or water (Sand Martin). The Swift feeds over any habitat.

SWALLOW

Lithe, elegant summer visitor, with distinctive long, forked tail, dark throat, and dark rump. Seen in the air or perched on wires or TV aerials; often nests in or on buildings. Makes distinct, liquid *swit-swit-swit* call.

↔ 17–19cm

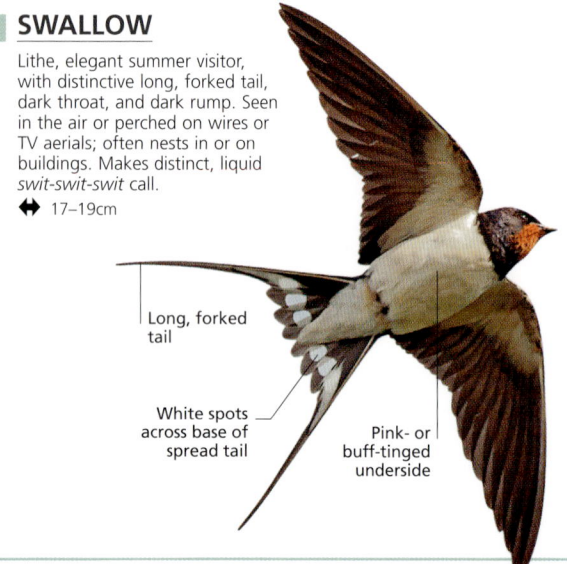

Long, forked tail

White spots across base of spread tail

Pink- or buff-tinged underside

HOUSE MARTIN

Small, aerial bird with characteristic white rump and underside. Builds mud nests under the eaves of buildings, or, more rarely, on cliffs.

↔ 12cm

Shiny, blue-black back

Blue-black cap

White rump above tail

White underneath, from chin to tail

What to look out for • Behaviour – perched or flying • Tail fork shape and length • Throat colour • Back and rump colour

SAND MARTIN

Tiny, aerial bird with distinctive, brown breastband. Makes long tunnels into earth or soft sandstone to nest. Often flies over water.

↔ 12cm

- Dark, triangular wings
- Short, notched, brown tail
- Pale underside
- Brown chestband

SWIFT

Long-winged and fork-tailed; minute legs and feet. Always in the air, except when at its nest, hidden in a cavity in a building or a cliff. Makes loud, screeching calls.

↔ 16–17cm

- Dull pale chin
- Brown-black all over
- Long, scythe-like wings

SPARROWHAWK
P.54

CHAFFINCH
P.21

Tree canopy
The highest twigs and branches of trees form a woodland "canopy". In some woods, the canopy is open; in others, such as beech woods, it is closed and lets little light in. A number of birds live in this habitat, including Chaffinches, Blue Tits, and Redpolls.

BLUE TIT
P.26

JAY
P.40

2 WOODLAND & FOREST

Forests are home to a mixture of insect- and seed-eating birds. These include woodland specialists such as woodpeckers, Nuthatches, and Treecreepers, which stay in the trees, as well as others such as pigeons, tits, and thrushes, which also feed outside the wood.

TREECREEPER
P.39

GREAT SPOTTED WOODPECKER
P.38

Bark

Large branches and tree trunks are home to insects, insect larvae, spiders, and other invertebrates, which provide food for woodpeckers and Treecreepers. Trees also offer good nest sites for birds that nest in cavities.

GOLDCREST
P.35

WILLOW WARBLER
P.34

Understorey

Mid-height branches, shrubs, and saplings provide dense cover and good feeding opportunities for birds such as Blackcaps, warblers, Goldcrests, and Blackbirds. Many birds also use the forest floor to feed or nest.

BLACKCAP
P.34

WOODLAND & FOREST

Small Woodland Birds

These birds of woodland, shrubs, and parkland are sometimes also found in gardens. Only the Chiffchaff, Blackcap, and Goldcrest are seen in the UK during winter.

CHIFFCHAFF

Small warbler, similar to Willow Warbler, but more drab, with an olive look and darker legs. *Chiff-chaff-chiff-chaff* song.

↔ 10–11cm

- Plain olive back
- Short wingtips
- Bobs tail frequently
- Pale half-circle under eye
- Dark legs

WILLOW WARBLER

A warbler of low woods and trees near heaths and moors. Paler and sleeker than Chiffchaff, with a sweet, warbling song.

↔ 11cm

- Pale greenish back
- Long wingtips
- Creamy yellow underneath
- Pale legs

BLACKCAP ♂

A warbler of woods and thickets; sometimes seen in big gardens in winter. Female has brown cap. Hard *tak* calls; song rich, fast, and warbling.

↔ 13cm

- Black cap
- Pale chin and throat
- Grey underside
- Brown wings

SMALL WOODLAND BIRDS

What to look out for • Leg colour • Tail colour • Head pattern • Presence of bars on wings

NIGHTINGALE

Plain, pale, red-brown bird of dense woods and low bushes. Famous for its song but secretive and shy.
↔ 16–17cm

- Brown back
- Pale ring and dark eye
- Rusty red tail

REDSTART ♂

Small, slender, Robin-like bird of woodland and nearby open spaces. Elusive in trees, but drops to the ground to feed, chasing insects with fluttering wings.
↔ 14cm

- White forehead
- Black bib (absent in female)
- Rusty underside
- Quivering red tail

GOLDCREST

Europe's smallest bird. Pale greenish in colour, with banded wings and plain face with striped crown that is visible close up. Often seen in conifers.
↔ 8.5–9cm

- Yellow stripe on black crown
- Broad white bar on wing
- Whitish face
- Pale body

Finches & Flycatchers

These small birds are commonly seen in forest clearings and parks (Spotted Flycatcher), and treetops (Pied Flycatcher, Crossbill, and Lesser Redpoll).

What to look out for • Head pattern and colour • Bars or flashes on wings • Streaks on upperparts and underside • Chin colour

CROSSBILL ♂

A stocky finch of conifer woods; eats conifer seeds, also some berries, buds, and insects. Seen on treetops, but often comes down to drink from puddles. Loud, jarring *jip jip jip* calls.

↔ 16cm

- Slightly pointed head
- Hooked beak
- Orange or red body
- Red rump

LESSER REDPOLL ♀

Small, slim, streaked finch. Female has red cap and black bib; male also has red chest. Often seen with Siskin (p.20) in noisy, mixed flocks around birch and alder trees.

↔ 11–14.5cm

- Red cap
- Black chin
- Buff bar on wing
- Plain brown tail

SPOTTED FLYCATCHER

Small, upright, short-legged but long-winged, summer bird. Often seen flying out from a low perch to catch insects in the air.

↔ 14cm

- Softly streaked crown
- Pale edges to wing feathers
- White below
- Very short, dark legs

PIED FLYCATCHER ♂

A summer bird of western oak woods; uses nest boxes. Flies out of foliage to catch flies in the air or insects on the ground. White wing panel bigger on males than females.

↔ 13cm

- Black upperparts
- Big, white wing panel
- White-edged tail
- White underparts

♀ see below

PIED FLYCATCHER ♀

More elusive and distinctly different from black-and-white male, but feeds in the same way, catching insects in the air or on the ground. Similar to female Chaffinch, but without shoulder patch.

↔ 13cm

- Brown back
- White wing panel
- Dull white underparts
- Short, dark legs

♂ see above

Bark Creepers

Woodpeckers cling to upright trunks and branches, Treecreepers creep up or cling beneath branches, and Nuthatches move freely in any direction.

What to look out for • Tail length and shape • Head pattern • Beak shape • Colour on rump and under tail

BLACK WOODPECKER

The biggest woodpecker. Similar to a slim Jackdaw (p.47) but with a red cap. Perches upright against tree trunks. Fast and direct flight. A continental European bird, not seen in the UK.

↔ 40–46cm

Red on crown or nape

Black body

Stiff black tail used as prop

GREAT SPOTTED WOODPECKER

A stunning, boldly patterned bird. Often seen at garden feeders. Known for its short, vibrant, spring "drumming" – made by hammering its beak against a tree. Loud *tchik!* call.

↔ 22–23cm

Red patch on head (not present on female)

Dagger-like beak

Big, oval, white shoulder patch

Bright red under tail

Stiff tail used as prop

BARK CREEPERS

GREEN WOODPECKER

Large, long woodpecker, with laughing call. Typical woodpecker flight pattern – deep, undulating action, then final, upward swoop to a perch. Often seen on the ground.
↔ 30–33cm

Black around eye
Red crown
Green back
Yellow rump

TREECREEPER

Always seen creeping on tree bark. Looks like a mouse as it climbs up a branch before flying down to start again on another one.
↔ 12.5cm

White below
Curved beak
Mottled brown back
Stiff, brown tail

NUTHATCH

This is a lively, active bird, common in woods and large gardens; often at feeders. Climbs without using its tail as a "prop" in the way that woodpeckers and treecreepers do.
↔ 12.5cm

Grey back
Black eye-stripe
Stout, dark beak
Reddish sides

Other Woodland Birds

The Jay is a woodland crow, the Hoopoe is a dazzling bird of open ground, the Cuckoo is heard more than seen, and the Tawny Owl is a nocturnal bird of woods and gardens.

JAY

A shy crow of woodlands, but can also be seen in parks. Collects acorns in autumn, then buries them to eat when food is scarce. Big, white rump is noticeable in flight. Often detected by its raucous, rasping call.
↔ 34–35cm

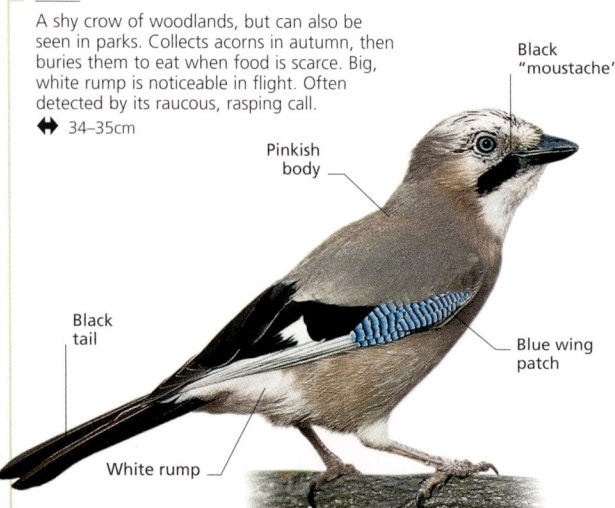

- Black "moustache"
- Pinkish body
- Blue wing patch
- Black tail
- White rump

HOOPOE

This is a strikingly patterned bird, rarely seen in the UK. It can be elusive as it walks on the ground in dappled light and shade. Found in warm and dry grassy or sandy places.
↔ 26–28cm

- Crest flat or fanned upright
- Long, thin beak
- Barred, black-and-white wings
- Barred tail

OTHER WOODLAND BIRDS | 41

What to look out for • Head shape and pattern • Back colour
• Tail shape and pattern

CUCKOO

A large, grey bird, with a spotted tail and drooping wings. More often heard than seen, but easy to find by following *cuc-ooo* song. Lays eggs in other birds' nests.

↔ 32–34cm

Grey back

Dark tail with white spots

Very short, orange legs

Barred underside

TAWNY OWL

Big-headed, with dark eyes. Often seen in gardens and parks. After dark, makes hooting calls and loud *ke-wick* notes.

↔ 37–39cm

Large, round head

Black eyes

Row of white spots on shoulder

Short, barred tail

3 OPEN COUNTRY

Modern farming methods mean fewer opportunities for birds, as they make fewer seeds and insects available. However, grassland, hedgerows, meadows, and less intensively cultivated fields all offer productive habitats for a variety of birds.

PHEASANT
Male, p.44

SKYLARK
P.49

JACKDAW
P.47

Open meadow

Grassland birds include the Grey Partridge, Jackdaw, Skylark, and Starling, which feed on insects, seeds, and worms at different times of year. Most feed their chicks high-nutrient insect food.

GREY PARTRIDGE
P.45

Skies

The open air should not be neglected as a habitat – Swifts and Swallows feed exclusively in the air, often over open farmland or moors, and Buzzards and Kestrels use the sky as an extra-high "perch" from which to see prey.

BUZZARD
P.56

Hedgerow

Some hedges have an abundance of berries, which are ideal for birds to eat in late summer, autumn, and early winter. Hedges are also great places for nesting for birds such as Rooks, Robins, Chaffinches, and Blackbirds.

ROOK
P.46

CHAFFINCH
P.21

BLACKBIRD
Male, p.24

YELLOWHAMMER
P.52

Gamebirds

These round-bodied, short-beaked birds are all chicken-like in general size and shape. They live in woods, fields and open spaces, and heather moors.

What to look out for • Tail length and shape • Plain or streaked back • Face colour and pattern • Tail colour in flight

PHEASANT ♂

A common bird released into wooded countryside and farmland in very large numbers for shooting. Many have white collars. Loud, crowing calls and sudden "whirr" of wings.
↔ 52–90cm

- Red face
- Green-black head
- Rusty or coppery body with black spots
- Very long, barred tail

♀ see below

PHEASANT ♀

Bigger than partridge and longer-tailed; shaped like the male but much less boldly coloured. Often seen at woodland edges.
↔ 52–90cm

- Plain, pale brown head
- Pale brown back with small black spots
- Pointed, barred tail
- Longer legs than partridge or grouse

♂ see above

RED-LEGGED PARTRIDGE

Pretty, rounded partridge with striking patterns, especially on the head. Common in Spain, introduced in other places. Loud, curiously mechanical, repetitive "chucking" calls.
↔ 32–34cm

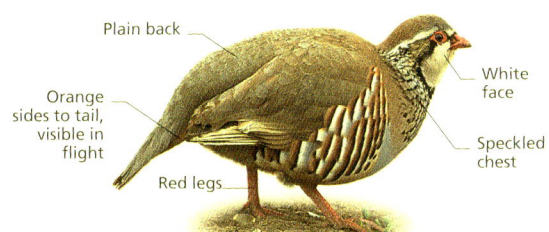

- Plain back
- White face
- Orange sides to tail, visible in flight
- Speckled chest
- Red legs

GREY PARTRIDGE

Less common than it used to be in farmland and open country. Small, streaked partridge, much more subtle in colour than Red-legged Partridge. Male's call a "creaky-gate" *kee-vick*.
↔ 29–31cm

- Orange face
- Grey neck
- Pale streaks on back
- Brown bars on sides
- Orange sides to tail, visible in flight

RED GROUSE ♂

Bird of heather moors. Overall very dark red-brown. Secretive, but bursts into flight if disturbed; loud, staccato *kooo-rr-rr-or or-or go bak bak bak* calls.
↔ 40cm

- Red over eye
- Very dark, red-brown body
- White-feathered legs and feet
- Black sides to tail, visible in flight

Crows

These thick-beaked and stout-legged birds are black or mostly black, and gather in groups. They are seen in open country, parks, and woodlands.

What to look out for • Tail length and shape • Shape and colour of beak, forehead, and face • Grey on neck or body

CARRION CROW

A big, black crow, much smoother-feathered than Rook and smaller and squarer-tailed than Raven. Found on open areas and in woodlands. Loud *caw* call.

↔ 44–51cm

- Thick, pointed, black beak
- Black body
- Glossy plumage
- Tightly feathered underside

ROOK

Big crow, with looser underside feathering, a much steeper forehead, and a sharper beak than Carrion Crow. Flies well, like a small Raven. Nests in treetop colonies.

↔ 44–46cm

- Black body, with blue and purple tones
- Bare white skin around base of beak
- Longer, rounder tail than Carrion Crow
- Loose, "baggy trousers" effect underneath

HOODED CROW

A grey-and-black version of the common Carrion Crow. Replaces Carrion Crow in places, including Scotland, the Isle of Man, Ireland, and parts of mainland Europe.
↔ 44–51cm

Black head and chest
Grey body
Shape like Carrion Crow
Black wings and tail

JACKDAW

Small, pigeon-like crow. Appears black but is actually mostly dark grey. Often mixes with Rooks on fields and in woodlands; also seen on old buildings.
↔ 33–34cm

Pale grey on back of neck
Black cap
Dark grey wings, with dull purple sheen in good light
Whitish eye

RAVEN

The world's biggest crow. Black body, like a giant Rook, with long wings and a rounded or diamond-shaped tail. Makes loud, echoing, throaty *crruk-crruk* and honking sounds.
↔ 56–57cm

Black plumage
Long, wedge-shaped tail
Throat feathers smoothed flat or raised in "beard"

Larks & Pipits

These are streaked, ground-loving birds. Larks are thicker-beaked and stockier than pipits. The Crested Lark is a continental European species not found in the UK.

MEADOW PIPIT

Slim, nervous bird, seen all year round. Smaller than a lark. Walks on the ground; *seep seep seep* flight calls. Pipits sing in the air, dropping like a shuttlecock with raised wings and tails.

↔ 14.5cm

- Slender, pointed beak
- Black streaks on cream underside
- Pale legs with long hind claws
- Soft streaks on brown back
- White edge to tail

TREE PIPIT

A summer bird. Similar to Meadow Pipit, but stockier and paler beneath. Streaks thick on breast but finer on sides. "Shuttlecock" flight like Meadow Pipit, finishing on a tree or a bush.

↔ 15cm

- Pale line over eye
- Black streaks on chest
- Thin streaks on sides
- Pale legs, with shorter hind claws than Meadow Pipit
- White edge to tail

ROCK PIPIT

Seaside equivalent of Meadow Pipit, but darker and greyer; yellower underneath with smudgier streaks. Flight call a slurred *tseep*.

↔ 16.5cm

- Wide dark streaks on yellow-buff underside
- Dark legs
- Greyish back with soft streaks
- Grey edge to tail

LARKS & PIPITS

What to look out for • Head shape, especially presence of crest • Upperwing colour in flight • Tail colour • Leg colour of pipits

SKYLARK

Smallish ground bird, bigger than pipit. Walks and rarely perches above ground, unlike Corn Bunting (p.52), which hops and perches on wires. Continuous song from high, hovering flight.

↔ 18–19cm

Short, blunt crest

White sides to tail

Pale edge on wing, visible in flight

Streaked breast above white belly

CRESTED LARK

Often seen on cornfields or waste ground. Looks orange-buff as it flies up; very short-tailed. Listen for loud, fluty *tree-loo-ee* calls.

↔ 17–19cm

Sharp, upright crest

Sharp streaks on chest

Sandy brown back

Buff sides to tail

Wings plain orange-buff underneath

WOODLARK

A scarce lark of heathland and scattered trees. More boldly patterned than Skylark. Beautiful, repetitive song from a circling flight or high perch.

↔ 15cm

Long eye-stripe to back of neck

Dark cheek patch

White-black-white patch on edge of wing

Whitish corners to tail

Chats & Warblers

Chats are found in open or bushy country, the warblers in low, tangled thickets, bushes, and hedges. Only the Stonechat remains in Europe all year round.

WHEATEAR ♂

Has big white patch above tail, obvious as it flies to a new, low perch. Keeps mostly to the ground on heaths, moors, and in grassy places.
↔ 14.5–15.5cm

Dark mask

Pale buff underside

Black "T" on tail tip

White tail sides and rump

STONECHAT ♂

Small bird of bushes, heaths, and coastal locations. Drops briefly to the ground to feed, but does not hop or run. Nervous *wheet-tac tac* calls.
↔ 12.5cm

Black head and throat (female lacks black throat)

White wing patch

White neck patch

Reddish breast

CHATS & WARBLERS

What to look out for • Head shape • Wing colour and pattern • Rump and tail colour and pattern • Chin and throat colour

WHITETHROAT

A small, slender, bright warbler with long tail. Likes thick undergrowth and hedges. Scolding, churring calls.
↔ 14cm

- Grey head
- Reddish wings
- White throat and pinkish breast
- Long tail with white sides

SUBALPINE WARBLER ♂

A small, pale bluish and pink warbler with slightly pointed head and longish tail. Found in dry, bushy places. A south European species, not seen in the UK.
↔ 12–13cm

- Blue-grey above
- White stripe below cheek
- Pink throat
- White-edged tail

Streaked Brown Birds

These triangular-beaked, seed-eating birds are found in open country; the Reed Bunting also inhabits wetlands. They all roam widely in countryside year-round.

CORN BUNTING

Stocky and big-billed. Similar to Skylark, but with plain wings and tail. Likely to perch on overhead wires or fenceposts. Song sounds like a bunch of keys being shaken.

↔ 18cm

- Streaked brown back
- Thick, pale beak
- Dark streaks on buff chest
- Brown tail

YELLOWHAMMER ♂

Slim, sharp-faced, and longer-tailed than Corn Bunting. Likes hedgerows and bushy places. Thin *si-si-si-si-si-seee* song in summer.

↔ 16cm

- Yellow head and chest
- Dark cheek stripes
- Black-and-white tail
- Rusty orange rump

STREAKED BROWN BIRDS | 53

What to look out for • Colour and pattern of head and chest
• Pattern of tail – white sides or flashes • Plain wings, or white-streaked in flight • Rump colour (reddest on Yellowhammer)

REED BUNTING ♂

Dark and streaked. Found in low thickets and damp places, mostly along watersides; also visits gardens. Female lacks black head and white collar. Simple, unmusical, jingling song.

↔ 15cm

Black, brown, and cream streaks on back

Black beak and head

White collar

Black-and-white tail

♀ p.88

LINNET ♂

Small, bouncy, lively finch. Female and winter male lack red patches. Found in small flocks in bushy heathland or on waste ground with low weeds. Light, twittering calls.

↔ 12.5–14cm

Grey head with red cap

Plain, ginger-brown back

Red patches on chest

White streaks on wings and tail

Small Birds of Prey

Among the varied birds of prey in Britain and Europe are sharp-winged falcons (Kestrel, Peregrine, Hobby), a blunt-winged hawk (Sparrowhawk), and two harriers.

KESTREL ♂

Small, common falcon of open countryside; not commonly found in gardens. Often perches on poles and wires. Sometimes hovers in one spot above the ground.
↔ 34–39cm

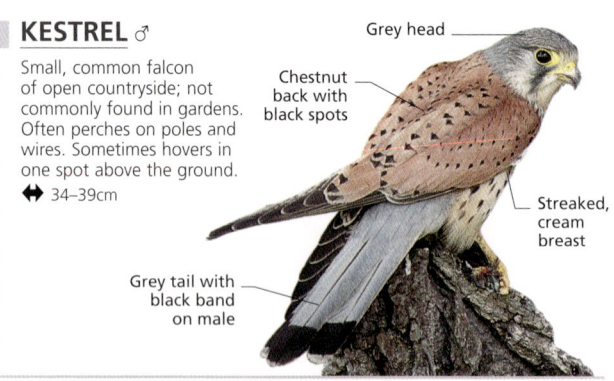

Grey head
Chestnut back with black spots
Streaked, cream breast
Grey tail with black band on male

SPARROWHAWK ♀

Small hawk; a common predator of woodland and farmland. Often seen dashing through gardens to take its prey (small birds) by surprise. Does not hover like Kestrel.
↔ 28–40cm

Short, blunt wings
Grey-brown back (male is blue-grey)
Barred, grey underside
Long, slim tail

HOBBY

Small, elegant falcon seen from April to September. Likes flying in the open air, above low-lying valleys, lakes, and heaths. Catches insects in flight.
↔ 28–35cm

Plain dark grey above
Black hood
White neck
Thick black streaks on underside
Red thighs

SMALL BIRDS OF PREY

What to look out for • Wing shape • Streaks or bars on underside • Head and cheek pattern, if any • Size and flight action

PEREGRINE

Large, broad-shouldered falcon of cliffs and large buildings. Catches pigeons and other birds in flight. Browner juvenile has dark streaks below.
↔ 39–50cm

- Black hood and "moustache"
- White neck and throat
- Pale grey back
- Grey bars on white underside

HEN HARRIER ♂

Large bird of prey. Flies low over heaths, moors, and marshes, gliding on raised wings. Female much browner than male.
↔ 43–50cm

- Black wingtips
- Grey head and body
- White rump
- Long, slim legs

HEN HARRIER ♀

Large bird of moors, heaths, and marshy places. Glides with raised wings. Males and females look distinctly different – females are larger and broader-winged.
↔ 43–50cm

- Owl-like head
- Dark brown back
- Banded tail
- White rump, visible in flight

Large Birds of Prey

This group of brown birds includes female harriers, one of the most common birds of prey (Buzzard), and two prized rarities (Red Kite and Osprey).

What to look out for • Tail colour and shape • Wing shape and flight action • Colour and pattern of rump and tail • Head pattern

RED KITE

A very large bird of prey. Its long wings are bowed or angled; tail with V-shaped fork looks sharply triangular when spread in flight.

↔ 60–65cm

- Pale head
- Big white patch near wingtip, visible in flight
- Rusty tail with fork, fans out in flight
- Rusty brown body

BUZZARD

Among the most common and widespread birds of prey. Seen in woods, farmland, and on moors. Soars on broad, raised wings.

↔ 50–57cm

- Large head
- Dark eye
- Broad cream U shape on chest
- Mottled brown body
- Barred, rounded tail

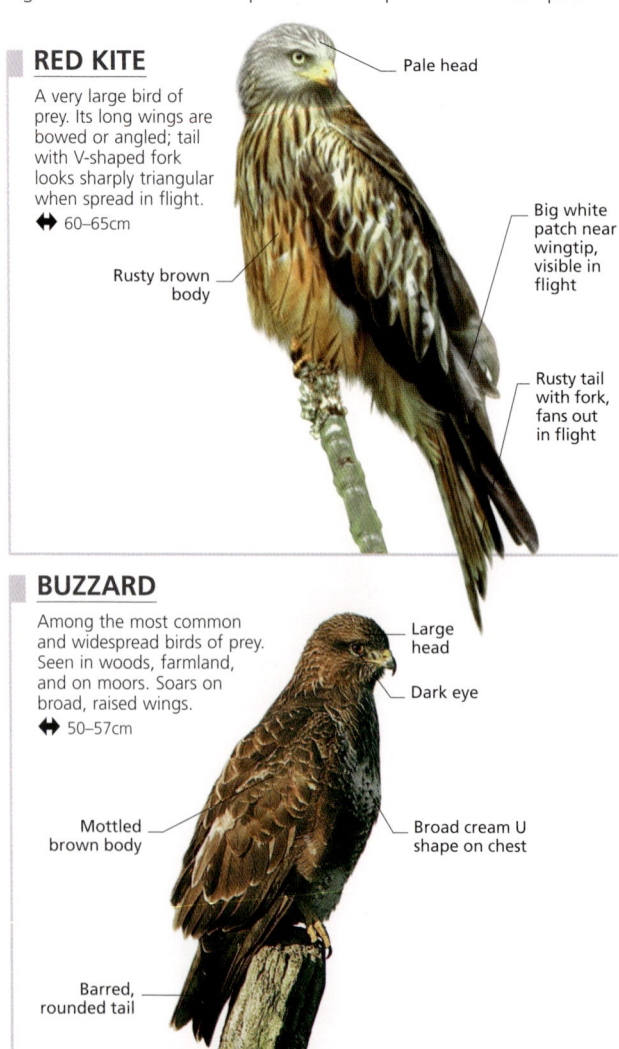

OSPREY

Rare bird of waterside woods and lakes; present from April to October. Often perches upright in big trees. Hovers over water and dives for fish.
↔ 52–60cm

White head
Black band behind eye
Dark brown back
White underside

MARSH HARRIER ♂

Large, broad-winged harrier of reed beds and wet places. Glides low on raised wings, but sometimes soars higher like Buzzard (p.56).
↔ 48–55cm

Dark brown back
Black wingtips
Grey tail
Pale grey wing patch

MARSH HARRIER ♀

The largest, darkest harrier. Has creamy head and wing marks. Usually found hunting low over reeds.
↔ 48–55cm

Plain brown body
Cream cap and throat
Plain brown tail

Birds of Prey

Birds of prey are large and impressive. They spend hours perched or soaring on warm air currents without using much energy. We see them most often in flight.

Identifying birds in flight can be difficult. It is hard to judge a bird's size against the sky, but looking at the flight action helps – is it light or heavy, fast or slow? Patterns, shapes, and postures are critically important because colours are difficult to make out on a flying bird.

WHAT TO LOOK OUT FOR

- Look at wingtip shape: is it pointed, blunt, straight, or swept back?
- Is the tail closed or fanned, square or rounded, notched or forked?
- Does the head protrude or look squat? Is it broad or narrow?
- Do the wings have curved or straight sides?
- Is the flight action stiff and jerky or relaxed and "elastic"?

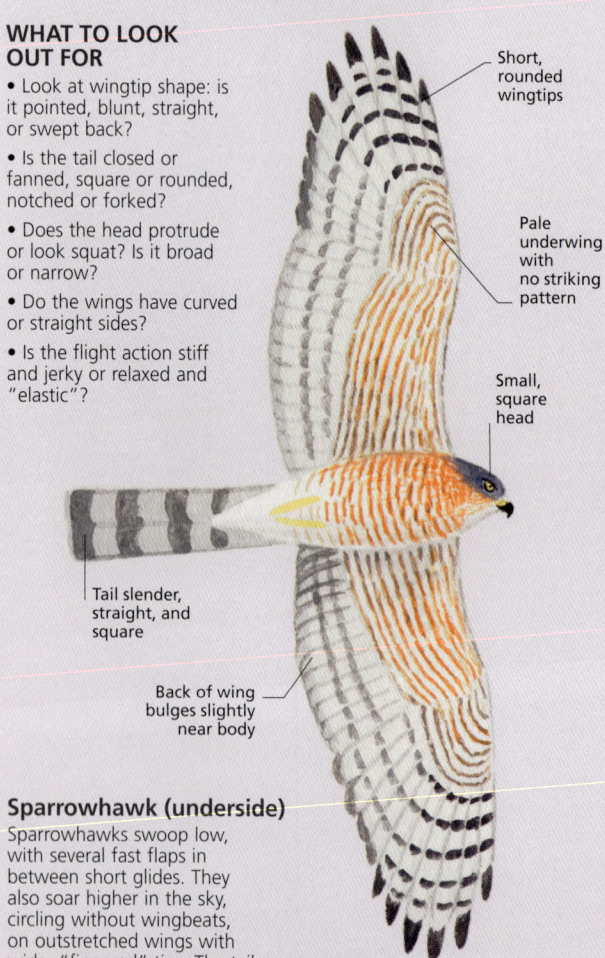

Short, rounded wingtips

Pale underwing with no striking pattern

Small, square head

Tail slender, straight, and square

Back of wing bulges slightly near body

Sparrowhawk (underside)

Sparrowhawks swoop low, with several fast flaps in between short glides. They also soar higher in the sky, circling without wingbeats, on outstretched wings with wide, "fingered" tips. The tail is long, slim, and square-cut.

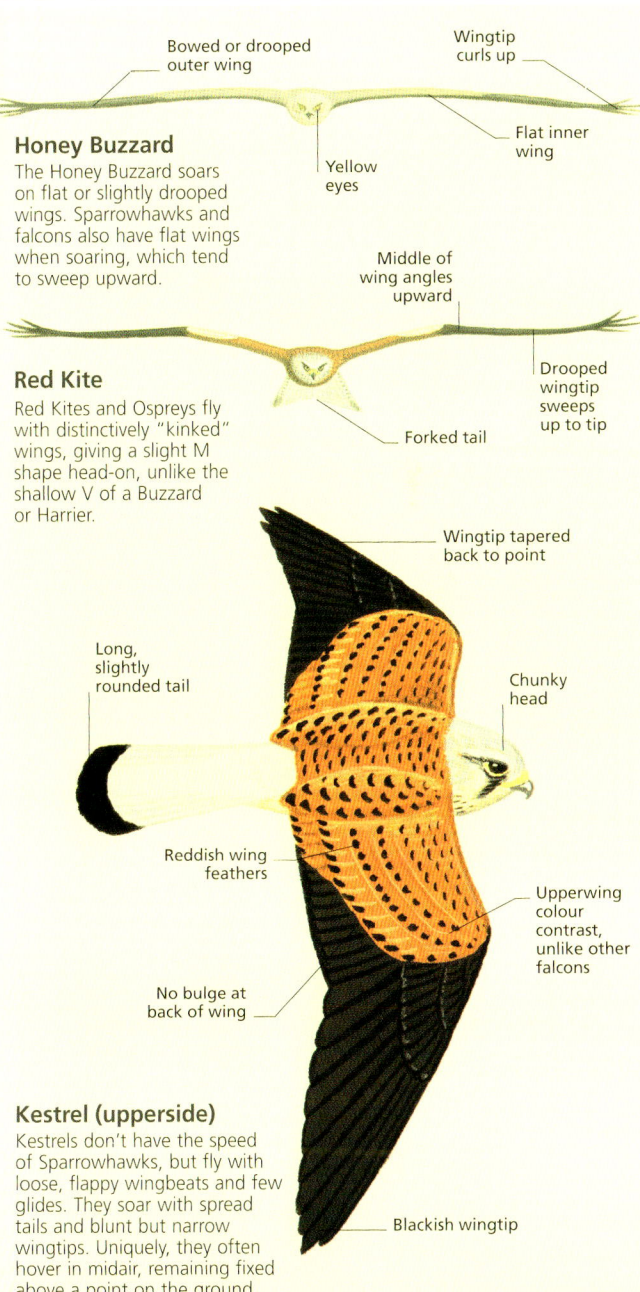

Honey Buzzard
The Honey Buzzard soars on flat or slightly drooped wings. Sparrowhawks and falcons also have flat wings when soaring, which tend to sweep upward.

Red Kite
Red Kites and Ospreys fly with distinctively "kinked" wings, giving a slight M shape head-on, unlike the shallow V of a Buzzard or Harrier.

Kestrel (upperside)
Kestrels don't have the speed of Sparrowhawks, but fly with loose, flappy wingbeats and few glides. They soar with spread tails and blunt but narrow wingtips. Uniquely, they often hover in midair, remaining fixed above a point on the ground.

SNIPE
P.80

LAPWING
P.78

Open shore

Wading birds such as the Snipe and Grey Heron find food on or within mud, sand, and silt, or in shallow water. Some birds sieve water for seeds and minute animal matter, while others probe the mud for worms, or hunt fish and frogs.

GREY HERON
P.76

4 WATER & WATERSIDE

Water adds great diversity to the habitats and food in a landscape, and so increases the number and variety of birds. If water is near woodland, swamp, or open ground, the landscape will be especially rich in wildlife.

KINGFISHER
P.88

GREAT CRESTED GREBE
P.72

MALLARD
Male, p.62

On the water
Some birds, such as the Coot, use open water as a safe refuge to sleep or rest. Others feed there, finding floating seeds and insects, or diving under water to find fish, shellfish, other invertebrates, or plants.

Reeds and sedges
Many water birds, such as the Moorhen, are secretive and need dense vegetation to feed or nest in; others come to these areas to roost at night. Reedy areas alongside water are always worth a long, close look.

MOORHEN
P.73

REED WARBLER
P.86

REED BUNTING
Female, p.88

Male Dabbling Ducks

These are surface-feeding (or dabbling) ducks that are at home on fresh water, salt water, and nearby marshes. The Mallard is common on ponds in parks.

MALLARD ♂

The most familiar park-pond duck, that comes easily for bread. Easily identified except in summer, when males are duller.
↔ 50–65cm

- Glossy green head
- Blue wing patch, edged white
- Grey body with brown bands

♀ p.64

GADWALL ♂

A large duck; greyer than Mallard and best identified by white wing patch in flight. Mostly found on fresh water.
↔ 46–56cm

- Pale, buff-grey head
- Grey-brown body
- Dark bill
- Black rear body

♀ p.64

SHOVELER ♂

Large duck with big, broad beak; easy to identify by its bold colours. Found on freshwater and coastal marshes, but not on the open sea.
↔ 44–52cm

- Green-black head
- Long, broad-tipped, shovel-like bill
- Reddish body
- White breast

♀ p.64

MALE DABBLING DUCKS 63

What to look out for • Head colour • Colour patch or stripes on back of wing • Leg and bill colours – grey or orange • Colour patch under or beside tail

WIGEON ♂

Neat, very short-legged duck. Often gathers in dense flocks on water or grazes on nearby grass; occurs both inland and on the coast. Loud, explosive, whistling call.

↔ 45–51cm

♀ p.65

Brown head with yellow forehead

Short, blue bill

Blue-grey body

Short, dark grey legs

Black and white by tail

TEAL ♂

The smallest duck. Although dark, its colours are visible at closer ranges in good light. Found inland and by the coast, often in muddy places.

↔ 34–38cm

♀ p.65

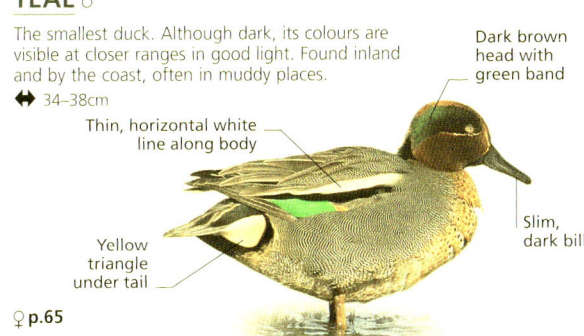

Dark brown head with green band

Slim, dark bill

Thin, horizontal white line along body

Yellow triangle under tail

PINTAIL ♂

Large, elegant duck. Long tail may be harder to see than the bold colours. Found in salt marshes and wet places inland. Most common in autumn and winter.

↔ 53–70cm

♀ p.65

Brown head with white neck stripe

Long, slender tail spike

Yellowish patch near tail

White chest

Female Dabbling Ducks

Male ducks are brightly coloured, but females are mostly brown. It is often possible to identify female ducks by the males they are accompanying.

MALLARD ♀

The biggest brown duck, with the loudest *quack quack quack* of all ducks. Has orange legs, and is common on park lakes and ponds.
↔ 50–65cm

Blue wing patch with white edges

Streaked, brown body

White tail

♂ p.62

GADWALL ♀

Similar to Mallard but slightly smaller and neater. Has orange legs. White wing patch visible in flight. Usually seen on freshwater lakes and rivers.
↔ 46–56cm

White patch on wing

Orange sides to bill

♂ p.62

SHOVELER ♀

Large duck with orange legs and a very broad beak, which is not so obvious at a distance. Dull blue shoulder patch visible in flight.
↔ 44–52cm

Dull patch on wing, visible in flight

Big, dark bill

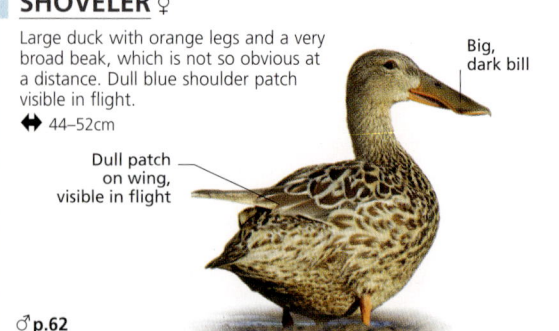

♂ p.62

FEMALE DABBLING DUCKS

What to look out for • Colour patch or stripes on back of wing • Bill colours • Streaks or patches on or near tail • Bill size and shape

WIGEON ♀

A shy bird, forming tight flocks on water. Has grey legs. Often feeds in dense flocks on dry ground near water. Makes low growling noise, rather than a "quack".
↔ 45–51cm

Round, brown head

Short, grey bill

Mottled rather than streaked

♂ p.63

TEAL ♀

A tiny, grey-brown duck with dark legs and bill. Often found on muddy watersides or flying fast in small groups.
↔ 34–38cm

White streak beside tail

Bright green patch on wing

Dark, mottled body

♂ p.63

PINTAIL ♀

Looks like a slim, long-necked Mallard, but with darker beak, dark grey legs, and a more pointed tail.
↔ 53–70cm

Pale brown head and neck

Grey bill

Pointed tail

♂ p.63

Male Diving Ducks

Diving ducks feed under water, plunging beneath the surface of the water as they swim. Male diving ducks are colourful, strikingly patterned birds.

TUFTED DUCK ♂

A lively diving duck, commonly found on ponds, lakes, and reservoirs. Males can be identified by their distinctive, drooping crest and bold, piebald colour scheme.
↔ 40–47cm

- Black head
- Yellow eyes
- Long tuft
- Blue bill
- Black body
- White sides

♀ p.68

POCHARD ♂

Often seen with Tufted Duck, but greyer, with distinctive head colour and a grey wing stripe. Less active and feeds more at night.
↔ 42–49cm

- Red-brown head
- Pale grey back and sides
- Dark from tail to rump
- Black chest

♀ p.68

GOLDENEYE ♂

Widespread but less common than Tufted Duck. Very active; often dives almost non-stop for long periods, on both sea and inland waterways.
↔ 42–50cm

- Bold, white spot on black face
- Black back
- Black-and-white wings
- White body

♀ p.68

MALE DIVING DUCKS 67

What to look out for • Head colour • Bill colour • White stripes, white patches, or grey bands on wing • Bill size and shape

GOOSANDER ♂

Large, long-bodied diving duck. Bigger than Red-breasted Merganser, with a simple but striking pattern. Found on freshwater lakes and rivers.
↔ 57–69cm

Hooked, dark red bill
Green-black head
Black back
White body

♀ p.69

RED-BREASTED MERGANSER ♂

A long-bodied diving duck. Similar to Goosander but with a more varied colour scheme and a more striking, spiky crest. Found on rivers, coasts, and large, sandy bays.
↔ 51–62cm

Blackish head with "double" spiky crest
Long, bright red bill
Grey body with white stripe on side
Dark chest

♀ p.69

EIDER ♂

Very large, heavy duck. Black-and-white in summer. Easily identified by its wedge-shaped head and beak. Found on sea coast and bays.
↔ 50–71cm

White head with black and green patches
Heavy, wedge-shaped bill
Black-and-white wings
Black underside

♀ p.69

Female Diving Ducks

Female diving ducks are plain in comparison to their male counterparts, with predominantly brown and grey bodies.

TUFTED DUCK ♀

Common freshwater diving duck. Mostly dark brown, with yellow eyes and a small "bump" on the back of its head. White stripe visible on open wing.
↔ 40–47cm

Small tuft

Grey bill with black tip

♂ p.66

POCHARD ♀

Grey-brown diving duck. Often gathers in mixed flocks with Tufted Ducks on freshwater lakes. Flocks are tightly packed, often made up largely of one sex.
↔ 42–49cm

Grey band along spread wing, visible in flight

Barred, grey-brown back

Whitish ring around eye

Long tapered bill

♂ p.66

GOLDENEYE ♀

Small, dark, rounded duck with a grey body and a dark brown head. Summer males look similar to females.
↔ 42–50cm

White patches on wing

Dark brown head

Short, triangular bill

♂ p.66

FEMALE DIVING DUCKS

What to look out for • Head colour • Bill colour – grey, orange, or red • Bill shape and size • White stripes, white patches, or grey bands on wing

GOOSANDER ♀

A bigger, more sharply patterned bird than the similar Red-breasted Merganser. Shy, easily frightened bird.
↔ 57–69cm

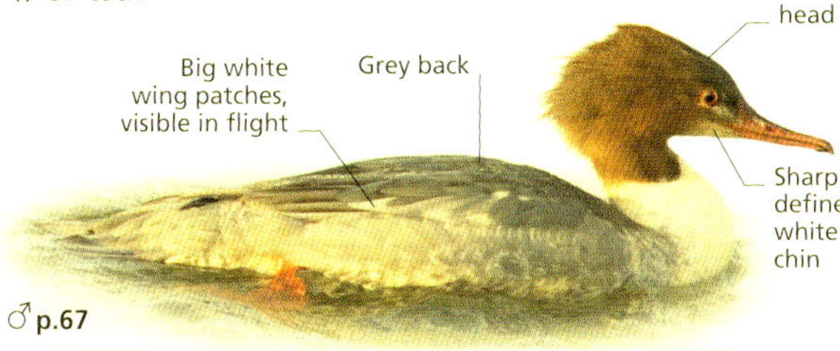

- Dark brown head
- Big white wing patches, visible in flight
- Grey back
- Sharply defined, white chin

♂ p.67

RED-BREASTED MERGANSER ♀

Browner plumage and a more smudged head and neck pattern than Goosander. Summer males and juveniles also have brown heads.
↔ 51–62cm

- Wispy crest
- Ginger-brown head
- Brownish grey body
- Slim, bright red bill

♂ p.67

EIDER ♀

A big, dark brown duck that is barred crosswise, rather than streaked lengthwise. Restricted to the sea, but often seen around coastal rocks and bays.
↔ 50–71cm

- Wedge-shaped head
- Barred body
- Short tail, often raised

♂ p.67

Ducks

Duck plumage varies depending on age, sex, and season. Breeding male, summer male, female, and juvenile birds can look quite different.

Duck breeding plumages are at their best through winter and spring, when ducks pair up to mate. After that, males moult to a dull eclipse plumage for the summer – at this time of year camouflage is more important than splendid colour.

MALLARDS

Even the common, tame Mallards of park lakes are worth studying closely. Although males and females share a basic size and shape, they look different, and the male plumage changes with the seasons.

White tail

Blue wing patch

Dark olive beak

Curly tail

Female
Mallard females are brown all year round but can be identified by features such as the bright blue wing patch (speculum), white tail, and leg and bill colours.

EIDERS

These ducks have a big, heavy appearance, with wedge-shaped heads and bills. You will only see them at the sea coast. The immature and female Eiders look very similar.

Wedge-shaped head

Female
The female Eider has a barred brown body and a paler head than the summer male, with a long wedge of facial feathers beside the thick bill.

Barred flanks

Immature
Young Eiders look much like females – they are barred crosswise, not lengthwise like most female ducks.

DUCKS

Summer male
Males in eclipse plumage look similar to females, but have redder feathers and yellow beaks. This male is halfway between eclipse and full breeding colours.

Head turns red-brown but in-between stages are frequent

Yellow beak

Winter male
Bright male Mallards in breeding plumage can be seen from late autumn to early spring. Their feathers are glossy and immaculate.

Green head

Yellow beak

White collar

Summer male
In non-breeding plumage the male Eider is mostly black-brown, with some paler patches and a pale streak behind its eye.

Pale eye-stripe

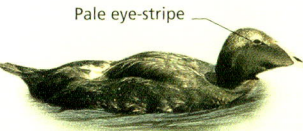

White back and flank patch

Pinkish chest

Winter male
In breeding plumage the male Eider is an unmistakeably pristine white, salmon-pink, and green.

Duck-like Birds

These are water and waterside species that can be seen throughout the year. They include rails (Moorhen and Coot), grebes, and a goose-like duck (Shelduck).

What to look out for • Beak and facial shield colour • Tail and rear end shape and colour • White stripes or patches on wing

GREAT CRESTED GREBE

Specialized diving bird; swims and dives like a duck but is not related. Has lobed (not webbed) toes and a dagger-like beak. Often found on the sea as well as freshwater lakes and rivers.
↔ 46–51cm

Sharp, pink beak

Black crest

Wide chestnut ruff

Bright white chest

LITTLE GREBE

Small, round, and almost tailless grebe. Frequently dives under the water. Mostly found inland, on rivers and lakes of all kinds. Has a loud, whinnying trill in summer.
↔ 25–29cm

Reddish cheeks

Black back

Very short tail

White spot at base of beak

DUCK-LIKE BIRDS 73

SHELDUCK

Strikingly white; visible at very long range. More goose-like than other ducks. Often walks across mudflats or swims on coastal pools and estuaries.

↔ 58–65cm

- Bright red beak
- White body
- Brown band around chest
- Pink legs

COOT

Appears very round-backed on water. On land, can be identified by its big, clumsy feet. A bird of fresh water, also feeds a lot on nearby open shores. Often gathers in large flocks.

↔ 36–38cm

- Black head and back
- Dark, grey-black body
- Low, rounded tail-end
- White face and beak

MOORHEN

Common, fairly secretive bird of fresh water and adjacent wet ground; creeps or flutters away if disturbed. Found in smaller groups than Coot.

↔ 32–35cm

- Red and yellow beak
- White flash under cocked tail
- Green legs and long, slender toes
- White stripe along side

Geese

These large birds are often found on or near water and in open fields. They are mostly sociable and some form flocks of many thousands in autumn and winter.

What to look out for • Beak and leg colour • Head, neck, and chest pattern • Contrast and pattern of wings in flight • Behaviour and location

CANADA GOOSE

A big, brown goose; often rather tame. Found on park lakes and town riversides. Introduced from North America; present all year round. Particularly loud, honking call in flight.

↔ 90–110cm

- Barred, brown body
- White chinstrap
- Black neck and head
- Pale chest

GREYLAG GOOSE

A big, grey-brown goose with very pale grey wings. Has distinctly coloured beak and legs. Found in wild flocks in the winter and also in semi-tame flocks year round.

↔ 74–84cm

- Orange beak
- Pale brown head and neck
- White around tail
- Pink legs

PINK-FOOTED GOOSE

Smaller and darker than Greylag Goose. Migrates from Iceland in large flocks. Found on coastal fields and marshes. Sharp *wink wink* call in flight.
↔ 64–76cm

- Small, dark beak with pink band
- Very dark head and neck
- Pale fawn chest
- Pink legs

BRENT GOOSE

The smallest and darkest goose. Found along low-lying coasts with fields and in estuaries. Often "upends" in salt marsh creeks, tipping forward so its head is under water, but tail is above.
↔ 56–61cm

- Black beak, head, neck, and chest
- Small white neck patch
- Dark or white belly
- Big, white area around tail

WHITE-FRONTED GOOSE

Best identified by its strong patterns and brightly coloured legs. Found on grassy meadows and marshes. Scarce in the UK, but common in northwest Europe during winter.
↔ 65–78cm

- White flash on forehead
- Pink beak
- Black bars on belly
- Orange legs

Large Waterside Birds

The heron, egret, and stork are tall, leggy waterside birds. Of the three swans, the Whooper and Bewick's are winter birds in Europe and breed in the far north.

GREY HERON

A very large, upright bird. Large and broad-winged in flight, with its wings deeply arched, and its long neck coiled back into the shoulders.
↔ 90–98cm

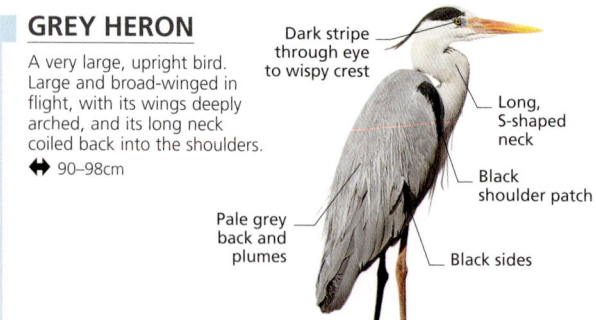

- Dark stripe through eye to wispy crest
- Long, S-shaped neck
- Black shoulder patch
- Pale grey back and plumes
- Black sides

LITTLE EGRET

Sparkling white heron, with "yellow slippers" on its long, black legs. Its numbers have increased almost everywhere, but it remains mainly close to the coast.
↔ 55–65cm

- Wispy back plumes in spring
- White head
- Sharp, dark beak
- Black legs
- Yellow feet

WHITE STORK

Huge bird of southern and central Europe. Very flat wings in flight, unlike Grey Heron's. Arrives in Europe in early spring, leaves for Africa in autumn. Flies in large, soaring, circling flocks.
↔ 0.95–1.1m

- White head and neck, often soiled
- Long, heavy, red beak
- Extensive black on wings
- Long, thick, red legs

LARGE WATERSIDE BIRDS

What to look out for • Beak colour and pattern • Position of head and neck in flight • Tail shape and length • Colour of legs and feet

MUTE SWAN

The common swan that comes for bread on park lakels; also lives on large lakes, rivers, and along the sea coast. Powerful flight, with neck outstretched. Present all year in most places.

↔ 1.4–1.6m

- Black and orange beak, with knob at base
- Wings often arched
- Beak usually held pointing downwards
- Slim, pointed tail, often raised

WHOOPER SWAN

A large wild swan, found from autumn to spring in most of Europe. Gathers in groups, sometimes mixed with other swans. Some found inland, but most are seen close to the coast.

↔ 1.4–1.6m

- Large, wedge-shaped head and beak
- Long, yellow triangle on beak
- Short tail, held low

BEWICK'S SWAN

Smaller version of Whooper Swan, best identified by its beak pattern. Flocks with Mute Swan, Whooper Swan, or both. Often on fields and marshes inland from late autumn to spring.

↔ 1.15–1.27m

- Rounded, yellow patch on side of beak
- Pure white all over
- Slightly shorter neck than other swans
- Short, flat tail

Wading Birds

These are all waders, but the Lapwing and Golden Plover prefer waterside or dry ground. The Grey Plover is an estuary bird; the Avocet likes mudflats.

LAPWING

Large bird, with a wispy crest and wide, rounded wings. Looks black and white at long range, greener close up. Often gathers in flocks on marshes and open fields.

↔ 28–31cm

GOLDEN PLOVER

Often mixes with Lapwings, forming large flocks on fields and grassy marshlands. The two species separate in flight, as Golden Plovers are faster and sharper-winged than blunt-winged Lapwings.

↔ 26–29cm

WADING BIRDS 79

What to look out for • Pattern beneath wing • Back colour and pattern • Head and face colour and shape • Beak size and shape

GREY PLOVER

Feeds mostly on mudflats and estuaries. Unlike Golden Plover, has black "armpits" and white rump, which are visible in flight. Less likely to mix with Lapwings and Golden Plovers; often seen with godwits, Curlews, and Redshanks.

↔ 27–30cm

- Round head
- Thick beak
- Speckled grey and black above
- Black face and underside in spring (dull white in winter)
- Black underside and base of wing

AVOCET

Scarce on coastal lagoons and muddy shores. Wades deeply, sweeping bill sideways as it feeds. White with bold black wingtips and stripes in flight.

↔ 41–45cm

- Curved black bands
- Upcurved bill
- Snow-white body
- Long, greyish legs

Brown Waders

These waders are brownish, except for the striking Oystercatcher. The Snipe is restricted to fresh water, and the Common Sandpiper prefers fresh to salt water.

GREEN SANDPIPER

A smallish wading bird; dark except for its white belly and rump. Appears more black-and-white in flight. Fluty, yodelling call.

↔ 21–24cm

Dark back with white specks
Pale stripe from beak to eye
Wing brown above, darker beneath
Pure white underneath

COMMON SANDPIPER

The brownest sandpiper, with a longer tail than most small wading birds. Bobs its head and swings its tail up and down while walking. Ringing *tswee-wee-wee* call.

↔ 19–21cm

Mid-brown above
Long, white wing stripe on brown wing, visible in flight
White "hook" in front of wing
Dull yellow-brown legs

SNIPE

A secretive bird of very wet, muddy places, as well as long grass or sedges. Flies up fast with a zigzag course. Call sounds like tearing cloth.

↔ 25–28cm

Striped back
Long, black and cream stripes on head
Short, rusty orange tail
Very long, straight beak

What to look out for • Wing and rump pattern in flight • Leg colour • Head and upperside pattern • Flight action and take-off behaviour – low or steep

OYSTERCATCHER

A big, black-and-white bird, easily identified by its striking appearance. Found on coasts, undisturbed fields, and riversides inland. Loud, piping calls.
↔ 40–45cm

Long, orange beak

Black-and-white body

Thick, pink legs

GREENSHANK

A scarce wading bird. Bigger and more elegant than Redshank. Seen most often in autumn, in most places. Loud, even *chew-chew-chew* call.
↔ 30–35cm

Long, slightly upcurved beak

Whiter around face and head than Redshank

Greyish brown back and wings

Greenish legs

REDSHANK

More common, smaller, browner, and usually noisier than Greenshank. Often found in large numbers on estuaries and wet areas inland. Ringing *tyew-yew-ew* call.
↔ 27–29cm

Brown head and body

Red and black beak

White patch on back of wing

Red legs

Coastal Waders

These waders tend to favour coastal habitats, but they can be seen inland on migration. Curlews and godwits are large, the others are smaller.

CURLEW

The largest wader. Gull-like in flight, but with longer legs. Looks plain and dark from a distance. Loud, beautiful *cur-lew* call; long, trilling song.

↔ 50–60cm

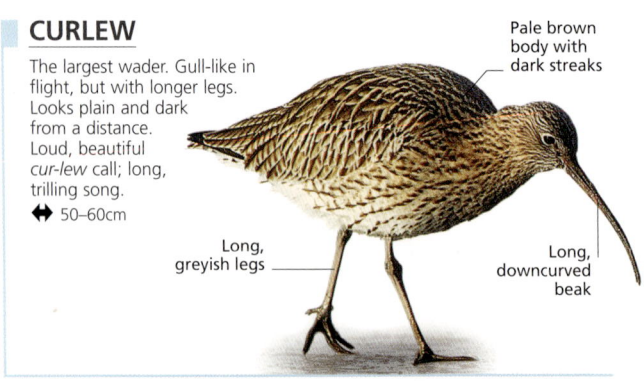

Pale brown body with dark streaks

Long, greyish legs

Long, downcurved beak

BLACK-TAILED GODWIT

A large wader, but much smaller than Curlew. Plainer and greyer than Bar-tailed Godwit in winter, with longer legs and a bolder pattern in flight.

Long, straight, pink and blackish beak

Coppery red from head to breast in summer (greyish in winter)

Broad, white stripe along wings, visible in flight

Long, blackish legs

↔ 36–44cm

BAR-TAILED GODWIT

A big, streaky brown wader. Found on large sand and mud estuaries and wide, open beaches, unlike Black-tailed Godwit, which prefers sheltered creeks.

↔ 33–42cm

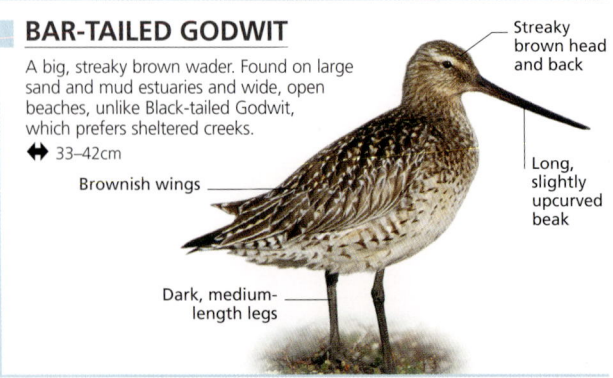

Brownish wings

Streaky brown head and back

Long, slightly upcurved beak

Dark, medium-length legs

COASTAL WADERS

What to look out for • Wing and rump pattern in flight • Beak length and shape • Leg length and proportions above and below the joint • Size – small, medium, large, or very large

DUNLIN

A common wading bird of muddy beaches; also appears by inland lakes in spring and autumn. Often in flocks. Distinctive *shrree* or *treerrr* call.
↔ 16–20cm

Streaked belly (black in summer)

Streaked, grey-brown head and back (brighter in summer)

Very dark legs

Thin, slightly curved beak

SANDERLING

A stockier, straighter-billed wader than Dunlin, with black legs. Also, much more restricted to open sandy or silty shores than Dunlin. Runs very fast beside the tideline.
↔ 20–21cm

Pale, silver-grey back (brown in summer)

Straight, black beak

Black legs

Very white beneath (never any black)

KNOT

Between Dunlin and Redshank (p.81) in size; medium-sized beak and legs. Plods rather than runs. Often seen in large flocks that fly with amazing coordination. Grey patch above tail visible in flight.
↔ 23–27cm

Short, straight beak

Dull grey in winter

Grey-green legs

Small Waders

These birds are found in different habitats: sea coasts (Turnstone), inland and on the coast (Ringed Plover), and by fresh water (Little Ringed Plover).

TURNSTONE

A smallish, stocky, thick-billed, orange-legged wading bird. Brightly coloured in spring, becomes darker in winter. Distinctive white wing and back patches visible in flight. Found on stony or rocky coasts, unlike other waders, which usually prefer soft ground such as sand or mud.

↔ 21–24cm

- Black-and-white head pattern (more black-brown in winter)
- White shoulder patches
- Black, white, and orange back (more black and brown in winter)
- Orange legs

LITTLE STINT

Tiny wader, smaller than a sparrow. In UK, an autumn migrant, mostly juveniles; adults in spring much scarcer. Has cream V shape on rusty back, which is most obvious from rear. Often seen with Dunlins (p.83) but can be told apart by its smaller size and whiter underside.

↔ 12–14cm

- Pale stripe over dark ear patch
- Black spots and buff scales above
- White underside

SMALL WADERS 85

What to look out for • Wing and rump pattern in flight • Leg colour • Pattern of head and upperside • Beak colour • Presence of eye-ring

RINGED PLOVER

Small, stocky waterside bird of salt- and freshwater coasts. Other "ringed" plovers have similarly patterned heads, but none in Europe have such a brightly coloured bill and legs. Call a liquid *tlu-ip!* note. White wing stripe visible in flight.

↔ 17–19cm

Black and white bands on head and chest

Orange-and-black beak

No streaks on brown back or white underside

Bright orange legs

LITTLE RINGED PLOVER

A small, sleek, "ringed" plover. Is only seen in Europe from spring to autumn, unlike Ringed Plover. Breeds at waterside or in dry, rough, open spaces. Makes a single, short *pew* note.

↔ 14–15cm

Yellow eye-ring

Plain wing (white stripe on Ringed Plover)

Black beak

Dull pinkish legs

Wetland Warblers

These are small birds of dense, waterside vegetation: reeds and willows (Reed Warbler), wet thickets (Sedge Warbler), and waterside thickets (Cetti's Warbler).

REED WARBLER

A summer bird. Plain brown above and buff beneath, with a whiter bib. Often found on reed beds; sometimes breeds in drier areas. Sings with a regular, repetitive, churring rhythm.
↔ 13–14cm

- Dark, spike-like beak
- Plain head
- White throat and chest
- Brown back
- Tail rustier than back

GRASSHOPPER WARBLER

Heard more often than seen; high, metallic, reeling trill, which is too high-pitched for some people to hear. Sings from low bramble or bush overgrown with long grass, or creeps quietly through dense vegetation.
↔ 12.5cm

- Softly streaked crown
- Soft, spotted lines on olive-brown back
- Longish, rounded tail
- Unmarked, yellowish-buff underside

WETLAND WARBLERS

What to look out for • Streaked or plain back • Head pattern • Neck and chest colour • Colour of rump and tail

SEDGE WARBLER

Best identified by its head pattern. A summer bird; found in nettles and bushy thickets by water more often than Reed Warbler. Varied, scolding, chattering song.

↔ 13cm

- Long, wide stripe over eye
- Soft streaks on back
- Pale underside
- Sandy brown rump

CETTI'S WARBLER

Present all year round. A very elusive, small, dark warbler of deep, waterside bushes and swamps. Best detected by its sudden, abrupt, loud, liquid burst of song.

↔ 14cm

- Thin eye-stripe
- Dark head
- Grey sides of neck and chest
- Dark, red-brown back and tail
- Broad, rounded tail tip

Small Waterside Birds

These birds include three wagtails that like wet or damp places; the Kingfisher, which must have clean, open water; and the Reed Bunting, a wetland or marsh bird.

What to look out for • Back and rump colour • Leg colour • Underside colour

KINGFISHER

Upright, dumpy shape and a long beak. Unique for its headlong dives (with a loud *plop*) into water. Often heard calling a loud, sharp *keee*, before a blue flash is seen dashing along a stream.

↔ 16–17cm

- Large, thick, dagger-like beak
- White throat and neck patch
- Blue above
- Orange below
- Vivid, electric-blue rump

REED BUNTING ♀

A small, finch-like bird. Has a long, black-and-white tail, and its back is heavily streaked with black. Stays close to the waterside in dense vegetation. Calls are short and high-pitched.

↔ 15cm

- Cream stripe over eye
- Black stripes on brown back
- Pale collar
- Fine streaks on white breast
- White sides to tail

♂ p.53

SMALL WATERSIDE BIRDS

PIED WAGTAIL ♂

Small, with a long tail. Easily identified by its black, white, and grey patterns. Walks fast and flicks its tail. Found on open ground, including car parks and roadside paths.
↔ 18cm

- Black cap
- Black neck
- Black or grey back (female greyer on back)
- Long black-and-white tail
- Spindly, black legs

GREY WAGTAIL ♂

Mostly grey and pale buffish in colour. Can be mistaken for Yellow Wagtail due to the yellow patch around the base of its tail. Present year-round, unlike Yellow Wagtail.
↔ 18–19cm

- Grey head and back
- Very long, black-and-white tail
- Yellow patch under tail
- Pale orange legs

YELLOW WAGTAIL ♂

The yellowest wagtail, with spindly, black legs and the least obvious, least wagged tail. Seen in Europe from spring to autumn.
↔ 17cm

- Yellow or grey head
- Pale line over eye
- Green back
- Unstreaked, yellow underside (female more buff)
- Thin, black legs

GUILLEMOT
P.100

SANDERLING
P.83

OYSTERCATCHER
P.81

Sheer cliffs

Cliffs provide secure nesting places for birds that live at sea, such as Guillemots and Kittiwakes. They also shelter nesting land birds such as Peregrines from disturbance and predators.

Sandy shore

Sand and shingle are easily swept or blown away, and make difficult places for tiny animals to live. This means that only a few birds feed on sandy shores, but many gulls, terns, and plovers nest on remote shingle banks.

5 COAST & SEA

Just as fresh water adds variety to the land, so the sea enriches any coastal habitat – even urban ones. Many birds can be seen from promenades and in coastal towns. The less disturbed areas of saltmarsh, estuary, and seacliff, however, are particularly rich in bird-life.

Estuaries

Occurring where rivers meet the sea, estuaries are a mix of fresh and salt water. They are rich and varied places; tides cover and expose mud and silt twice a day, bringing nutrients for the invertebrates that live there, and creating opportunities for birds to feed on them.

REDSHANK
P.81

SHAG
P.102

GANNET
P.102

FULMAR
P.95

At sea

Seabirds are wonderfully adapted to a tough ocean life. They can be seen flying past headlands, especially during heavy winds, but to see them truly at home in this demanding environment, it is best to get out in a boat.

Muddy shore

The weighty stability of mud and the rich nutrients brought in by the tides mean that muddy shores, creeks, and estuaries are much better for most birds than sand. However, at high tide, waders such as the Knot need to find safe refuge elsewhere.

SHELDUCK
P.73

KNOT
P.83

Large Gulls

These common, noisy, and large water birds are mostly white and grey. They fly well, soaring high, and are good swimmers, but are just as at home on dry land.

HERRING GULL

The typical, noisy gull spotted on rooftops, promenades, and beaches. A bossy and aggressive bird; head turns grey-brown in winter. Pale eyes, unlike Common Gull (p.94).

↔ 55–67cm

- Red spot on yellow beak
- Pale eye
- White head in summer
- Pale grey back
- Black wingtips with white spots
- Pink legs

LESSER BLACK-BACKED GULL

As big as Herring Gull, but slimmer; much smaller than Great Black-backed Gull. Head smudged grey-brown in autumn–winter. Gathers in large flocks.

↔ 52–67cm

- Head white in summer
- Dark grey back
- Slender, black-and-white wingtips
- Yellow legs

LARGE GULLS

What to look out for • Size – large or very large (Great Black-backed Gull) • Beak and leg colour, which may change with seasons • Wingtip patterns, especially on open wings • Back and wing colour, from pale grey to black; juveniles brown

GREAT BLACK-BACKED GULL

The biggest gull; dramatic in flight and impressively well-built on the ground. Less common than other gulls, but very widespread.
↔ 64–78cm

- White head
- Yellow bill with red spot
- Black back and wings
- Pale pink legs

YELLOW-LEGGED GULL

Similar to Herring Gull, but with a slightly darker back, and a white head in winter as well as in summer. Mainly found in the Mediterranean region.
↔ 55–65cm

- White head
- Smooth, mid-grey back
- Long, black-and-white wingtips
- Yellow legs

Small Gulls & Fulmar

Gulls divide their time between sea and land, except the Kittiwake, which only comes to land to nest. The Fulmar looks like a gull, but is not related to them.

What to look out for • Back, rump, and tail colour • Beak and leg colour • Wingtip patterns, especially in flight • Head pattern

BLACK-HEADED GULL

Common, noisy, squabbling gull. Small, very pale, with broad, white flash on the front of open wings. Beak and legs deep red in summer, brighter in winter. White head with brown hood in summer.
↔ 34–37cm

Brown hood in summer, at other times head white with black ear spot or patterns

Dark red beak

Black-tipped wings

White flash along edge of wing

Red legs

COMMON GULL

Similar to small, dark Herring Gull (p.92), but with different leg and beak colours, and gentle, dark eye. Often found on grassy fields and muddy beaches.
↔ 38–44cm

Mid-grey back

Small, greenish yellow beak

Large, black-and-white wingtips

Green legs

SMALL GULLS & FULMAR

MEDITERRANEAN GULL

A once scarce bird that is now increasing in number. Similar to Black-headed Gull but paler, with pure white underwing and pearly grey upperwing.

↔ 36–38cm

Jet-black hood in summer, white head with dark eye-patch in winter

Bright red beak

Unmarked white wingtips

Red or blackish legs

KITTIWAKE

Seagoing gull, seen on coastal cliffs but not inland. Similar to small, delicate Common Gull but has very short, black legs. Juvenile has black zigzag pattern on wings. Calls loud *kitti-a-wa-ake* from cliffs or ledges on coastal buildings.

↔ 38–40cm

Dark eye

Small, yellowish beak

Unmarked, black wingtips

Short, blackish legs

FULMAR

Gull-like seabird of cliffs and open seas, but not related to gulls. Cannot stand or walk due to weak legs, but is a very strong flier on stiff wings.

↔ 45–50cm

Big, white head

Large, dark eye

Stubby, hooked, grey-and-yellow beak

Patchy, grey wings

Grey tail

Gulls

Large gulls take several years to mature fully. As they get older their plumage changes, making it possible to tell the ages of different individuals.

Changes in plumage come about when birds moult – old feathers fall out and new ones grow. Gulls start off brown and become pale grey, white, and black with age. After four years, adult gulls alternate between breeding (summer) and non-breeding (winter) plumage – look for changes in spring and late summer/autumn. The birds shown here are all Herring Gulls.

Blackish beak

Sharp black wingtips with white spots

Dark bars on back

Black wingtips and tail band

First year
A gull's first feathers are its brownish juvenile plumage. In its first autumn, a gull moults into its first winter plumage. It moults again in spring into its first summer plumage. The beak remains almost black.

Yellow-and-black beak

Extensive grey on wings and back

White underparts

Third year
In the second and third years, all feathers change each autumn, and head and body feathers change again each spring, making the young gull look progressively more like an adult.

GULLS

Summer adult
After four years, it is impossible to tell a Herring Gull's precise age by its plumage. However, breeding and non-breeding plumages alternate by season. In summer, an adult gull has a pure white head and bright beak and leg colours.

- Pale eye with orange ring
- Bright yellow beak with red spot
- Grey back and wings
- White chest and head

Winter adult
In the winter, adult Herring Gulls have brown-streaked heads. The streaked head and breast return to white in spring.

- Eye-ring less orange than in summer
- Heavily streaked head and breast
- Body same as in summer

Terns

Most terns are seabirds, but the Common Tern is equally at home inland. Terns are long-distance migrants – they fly south in autumn and return in spring.

COMMON TERN

A sleek, slender bird. Similar to Arctic Tern but paler, longer-legged, and with a more southerly distribution. Found on coasts, inland lakes, and rivers.

↔ 31–35cm

- Black cap
- Red beak with black tip
- Long, dark-streaked wingtips
- Red legs
- Very pale grey beneath

ARCTIC TERN

More strictly a seabird than Common Tern, with shorter legs and a shorter, spikier beak. Outer wing translucent in flight. Nests on rocky islands. Migrates past southern coasts on its way to Southern Ocean in spring and autumn.

↔ 32–35cm

- Red beak
- Black cap
- Grey back
- Silvery grey wingtips
- Mid-grey beneath
- Red legs

What to look out for • Beak and leg colour and pattern
• Wingtip pattern in flight, above and below • Leg length

SANDWICH TERN

The largest among the most widespread terns, and the palest. Often seen fishing in sandy, coastal bays, diving in with a big splash. Raucous *kier-ink* call.

↔ 36–41cm

Long, black beak with pale tip

Very pale, silvery grey back

White beneath

Black legs

LITTLE TERN

The tiniest tern. Usually seen on the coast, flying fast and dashing into the sea for small fish. Rare bird of sand and shingle beaches.

↔ 22–24cm

Sharp, white forehead

Black cap

Spiky, yellow beak

Greyish black wingtips

Yellow or orange legs

White beneath

Specialist Seabirds

Strictly seabirds, these auks rarely come to land, except to nest on cliffs. The Black Guillemot nests on rocky islets in more northerly locations.

PUFFIN

Small, upright bird of coastal cliffs and islands, or the open sea. Nests in cavities high on cliffs. Scarce off headlands away from its nesting sites. Flies low and fast over the waves.
↔ 26–29cm

- Triangular, multicoloured beak
- Round head with grey cheeks
- Black chestband and back
- Orange legs

GUILLEMOT

A slim, sharp-beaked seabird. Nests on ledges and on the tops of offshore rocks near the coast. Swims or flies fast and low over the sea.
↔ 38–54cm

- Pointed, dagger-like beak
- Dark brown back and wings
- White belly
- Short, square tail

SPECIALIST SEABIRDS | 101

What to look out for • Beak shape, colour, and pattern
• Leg colour • Presence of wing patch • Nesting site location

RAZORBILL

Stockier and thicker-billed than Guillemot. Found on the open sea or sea cliffs in summer. Nests in cavities high on cliffs. Swims in close flocks in larger estuaries.

↔ 37–39cm

Black head, neck, and back

Thick, hooked beak with white lines

White belly

Pointed, black tail

BLACK GUILLEMOT

Smaller than Guillemot. Plumage is mottled much whiter in winter than in summer. Nests on low, rough boulders in rocky islets and on cliffs. Seen around coasts more often than Guillemot.

↔ 30–32cm

Smoky black head and body

White wing patch

Short, pointed beak

Short, red legs

Large Seabirds

In this group only the Cormorant goes inland, nesting on trees and coastal cliffs. The Gannet nests in dense colonies, and the Shag in smaller groups on the coast.

What to look out for • Face pattern, especially cheek and fleshy pouch by the beak

GANNET

Extremely large seabird. Young are dark at first, becoming patchy white with age. Seen in wide bays or off rocky headlands, but not inland. Dives into the sea from a great height.
↔ 85–89cm

- Dagger-like beak on long head
- Brilliant white plumage
- Triangular, black wingtips
- Pointed, white tail

CORMORANT

A big, dark swimming bird with a long, hooked beak. Flies with deep, quick wingbeats like a goose, but much blacker and with a longer tail. Often stands with half-open wings. Seen just as often inland as on the coast.
↔ 80–100cm

- White cheek patch
- Blackish overall
- Short, thick legs
- Long, wide tail

SHAG

Slightly smaller, neater, and snakier than Cormorant, with a rounder head, steeper forehead, and slimmer beak. Strictly a seabird, very rare inland.
↔ 65–80cm

- Short crest
- Yellow patch at base of beak
- Greenish black plumage
- Wide tail

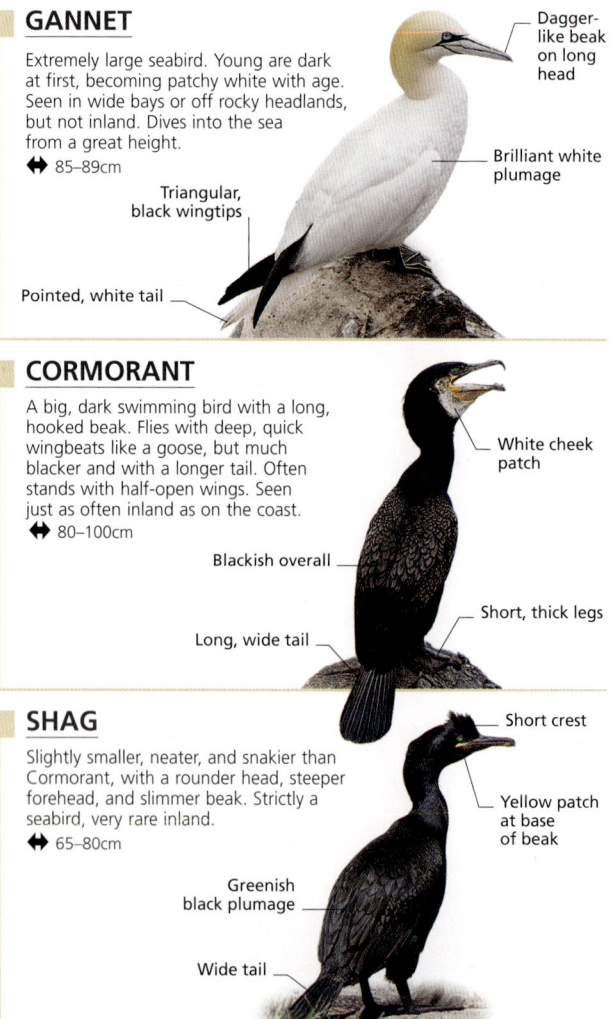

BIRD GALLERY

This colour gallery shows the birds already profiled in the book, grouped by colour. When you see a bird, flick through the colour groupings to find options most like the bird you are watching, then go to their profile page for a closer look and important identification details. Some birds appear in more than one colour grouping.

Size guide
Birds are grouped in four sizes. Apparent size is more a function of "bulk" than length, so these groups are not precise – but they can help you figure out what you are looking at.

COLOUR GROUP

TINY (House Sparrow) SMALL (Town Pigeon)

MEDIUM (Mallard) LARGE (Mute Swan)

Contents

104–105	White; Grey
106–107	Grey (continued); Black, white, and grey; Black and white
108–109	Black and white (continued); Black
110–111	Black (continued); Brown; Brown: streaked, spotted, or barred
112–113	Brown: streaked, spotted, or barred (continued)
114–115	Brown: streaked, spotted, or barred (continued); Red, orange, or pink
116–117	Red, orange, or pink (continued); Green
118–119	Blue patches; Rufous on tail/rump; Yellow
120–121	Brown waders; Grey-and-white waders; Black-and-white waders

BIRD GALLERY

WHITE
For gulls, see
pp.106–107

Mute Swan
p.77

Whooper Swan
p.77

GREY
For grey-and-white
waders, see pp.120–121

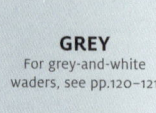

Grey Wagtail ♂
p.89

Wheatear ♂
p.50

Woodpigeon
p.28

Stock Dove
p.29

Town Pigeon
p.28

Goldeneye ♀
p.68

Goosander ♀
p.69

Red-breasted Merganser ♀
p.69

Gadwall ♂
p.62

Mallard ♂
p.62

Hen Harrier ♂
p.55

BIRD GALLERY

Bewick's Swan
p.77

Little Egret
p.76

White Stork
p.76

Nuthatch
p.39

Bullfinch ♂
p.21

Collared Dove
p.29

Cuckoo
p.41

Hooded Crow
p.47

Teal ♂
p.63

Pochard ♂
p.66

Pintail ♂
p.63

Wigeon ♂
p.63

Grey Heron
p.76

Black-headed Gull
p.94

Herring Gull
p.92

106 | BIRD GALLERY

GREY (CONTINUED)

Common Gull
p.94

Kittiwake
p.95

BLACK, WHITE, AND GREY

Red-breasted Merganser ♂
p.67

Little Tern
p.99

Black-headed Gull
p.94

Mediterranean Gull
p.95

Common Gull
p.94

Yellow-legged Gull
p.93

Pied Wagtail ♂
p.89

Peregrine
p.55

BLACK AND WHITE

For more black-and-white waders, see pp.120–121

Coal Tit
p.27

Long-tailed Tit
p.27

BIRD GALLERY | 107

Fulmar
p.95

Common Tern
p.98

Arctic Tern
p.98

Sandwich Tern
p.99

Lesser Black-backed Gull
p.92

Kittiwake
p.95

Herring Gull
p.92

Hobby
p.54

Pied Flycatcher ♂
p.37

House Martin
p.30

Stonechat ♂
p.50

108 | BIRD GALLERY

BLACK AND WHITE (CONTINUED)

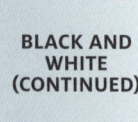
Great Spotted Woodpecker
p.38

Magpie
p.25

Razorbill
p.101

Puffin
p.100

Guillemot
p.100

Great Black-backed Gull
p.93

Gannet
p.102

Goldeneye ♂
p.66

Coot
p.73

Brent Goose
p.75

Canada Goose
p.74

BLACK

Blackbird ♂
p.24

Starling
p.24

BIRD GALLERY 109

110 | BIRD GALLERY

BLACK (CONTINUED)

Carrion Crow
p.46

Raven
p.47

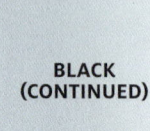
Cormorant
p.102

BROWN

Marsh Tit
p.27

Swift
p.31

Pied Flycatcher ♀
p.37

Reed Warbler
p.86

Nightingale
p.35

Jay
p.40

Little Grebe
p.72

BROWN: STREAKED, SPOTTED, OR BARRED

Wren
p.19

Treecreeper
p.39

BIRD GALLERY | 111

Black Woodpecker
p.38

Shag
p.102

Cormorant
p.102

Sand Martin
p.31

Waxwing
p.25

Swift
p.31

Whitethroat
p.51

Tufted Duck ♀
p.68

Nightingale
p.35

Dunnock
p.18

Spotted Flycatcher
p.37

House Sparrow ♂
p.18

BIRD GALLERY

BROWN: STREAKED, SPOTTED, OR BARRED (CONTINUED)

House Sparrow ♀
p.18

Tree Sparrow
p.19

Skylark
p.49

Crested Lark
p.49

Blackbird ♀
p.23

Sedge Warbler
p.87

Grasshopper Warbler
p.86

Linnet ♂
p.53

Yellowhammer ♂
p.52

Song Thrush
p.22

Mistle Thrush
p.22

Mallard ♀
p.64

Gadwall ♀
p.64

Shoveler ♀
p.64

BIRD GALLERY | 113

Meadow Pipit
p.48

Tree Pipit
p.48

Rock Pipit
p.48

Woodlark
p.49

Stonechat ♂
p.50

Reed Bunting ♂
p.53

Lesser Redpoll ♀
p.36

Corn Bunting
p.52

Reed Bunting ♀
p.88

Redwing
p.23

Fieldfare
p.23

Turtle Dove
p.29

Wigeon ♀
p.65

Teal ♀
p.65

Pintail ♀
p.65

114 | BIRD GALLERY

BROWN: STREAKED, SPOTTED, OR BARRED (CONTINUED)

Pochard ♀
p.68

Eider ♀
p.69

Pheasant ♀
p.44

Red-legged Partridge
p.45

Grey Partridge
p.45

Red Kite
p.56

Tawny Owl
p.41

Osprey
p.57

Canada Goose
p.74

Marsh Harrier ♂
p.57

RED, ORANGE, OR PINK

Subalpine Warbler ♂
p.51

Chaffinch ♂
p.21

Brambling ♂
p.21

BIRD GALLERY

Kestrel ♂ p.54	 Sparrowhawk ♀ p.54	 Pheasant ♂ p.44
 Red Grouse ♂ p.45	 Hen Harrier ♀ p.55	 Buzzard p.56
 Greylag Goose p.74	 Pink-footed Goose p.75	 White-fronted Goose p.75
 Robin p.19	 Redstart ♂ p.35	 Stonechat ♂ p.50

Bullfinch ♂
p.21

Redwing
p.23

Linnet ♂
p.53

116 | BIRD GALLERY

RED, ORANGE, OR PINK (CONTINUED)

Lesser Redpoll ♀
p.36

Crossbill ♂
p.36

Red Grouse ♂
p.45

Pochard ♂
p.66

Wigeon ♂
p.63

Hoopoe
p.40

GREEN

Greenfinch
p.20

Goldcrest
p.35

Blue Tit
p.26

Great Tit
p.26

Yellow Wagtail ♂
p.89

Starling
p.24

Lapwing
p.78

BIRD GALLERY 117

Nuthatch
p.39

Kingfisher
p.88

Waxwing
p.25

Little Grebe
p.72

Great Crested Grebe
p.72

Turtle Dove
p.29

Shoveler ♂
p.62

Mallard ♂
p.62

Green Woodpecker
p.39

Chiffchaff
p.34

Willow Warbler
p.34

Siskin ♂
p.20

Teal ♂
p.63

Goosander ♂
p.67

Pheasant ♂
p.44

BIRD GALLERY

BLUE PATCHES

Blue Tit
p.26

Kingfisher
p.88

Swallow
p.30

Jay
p.40

RUFOUS ON TAIL/ RUMP

Redstart ♂
p.35

Nightingale
p.35

YELLOW

Goldfinch
p.20

Siskin ♂
p.20

Yellowhammer ♂
p.52

Blue Tit
p.26

Great Tit
p.26

BIRD GALLERY 119

House Martin
p.30

Moorhen
p.73

Mallard ♀
p.64

Crossbill ♂
p.36

Yellowhammer ♂
p.52

Red kite
p.56

Greenfinch
p.20

Goldcrest
p.35

Grey Wagtail ♂
p.89

Willow Warbler
p.34

Yellow Wagtail ♂
p.89

120 | BIRD GALLERY

BROWN WADERS
For other brown birds
see pp.112–117

Snipe
p.80

Golden Plover
p.78

Greenshank
p.81

Redshank
p.81

Curlew
p.82

Little Stint
p.84

Ringed Plover
p.85

Turnstone
p.84

GREY-AND-WHITE WADERS
For other grey birds,
see pp.104–105

Sanderling
p.83

Knot
p.83

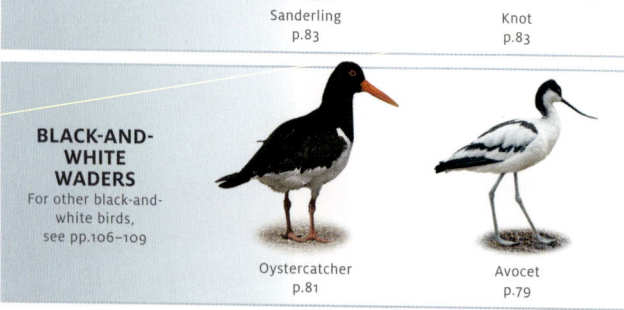

BLACK-AND-WHITE WADERS
For other black-and-white birds,
see pp.106–109

Oystercatcher
p.81

Avocet
p.79

BIRD GALLERY | 121

Green Sandpiper
p.80

Common Sandpiper
p.80

Dunlin
p.83

Black-tailed Godwit
p.82

Bar-tailed Godwit
p.82

Little Ringed Plover
p.85

Greenshank
p.81

Grey Plover
p.79

Grey Plover
p.79

Ringed Plover
p.85

Lapwing
p.78

Scientific Names

Every living species has a scientific name of two words derived from Latin or Greek. The first word is the genus, shared by closely related species that often look similar. The second is the specific name. Each two-word combination is unique to the individual species.

Common name	Scientific name	Page
Dunnock	*Prunella modularis*	18
House Sparrow	*Passer domesticus*	18
Tree Sparrow	*Passer montanus*	18
Robin	*Erithacus rubecula*	19
Wren	*Troglodytes troglodytes*	19
Goldfinch	*Carduelis carduelis*	20
Greenfinch	*Carduelis chloris*	20
Siskin	*Carduelis spinus*	20
Chaffinch	*Fringilla coelebs*	21
Bullfinch	*Pyrrhula pyrrhula*	21
Brambling	*Fringilla montifringilla*	21
Song Thrush	*Turdus philomelos*	22
Mistle Thrush	*Turdus viscivorus*	22
Redwing	*Turdus iliacus*	23
Fieldfare	*Turdus pilaris*	23
Blackbird	*Turdus merula*	23, 24
Starling	*Sturnus vulgaris*	24
Waxwing	*Bombycilla garrulus*	25
Magpie	*Pica pica*	25
Great Tit	*Parus major*	26
Blue Tit	*Cyanistes caeruleus*	26
Coal Tit	*Periparus ater*	27
Long-tailed Tit	*Aegithalos caudatus*	27
Marsh Tit	*Poecile palustris*	27
Town Pigeon	*Columba livia*	28
Woodpigeon	*Columba palumbus*	28
Stock Dove	*Columba oenas*	29
Collared Dove	*Streptopelia decaocto*	29
Turtle Dove	*Streptopelia turtur*	29
Swallow	*Hirundo rustica*	30
House Martin	*Delichon urbicum*	30
Sand Martin	*Riparia riparia*	31
Swift	*Apus apus*	31
Chiffchaff	*Phylloscopus collybita*	34
Willow Warbler	*Phylloscopus trochilus*	34
Blackcap	*Sylvia atricapilla*	34
Nightingale	*Luscinia megarhynchos*	35
Redstart	*Phoenicurus phoenicurus*	35
Goldcrest	*Regulus regulus*	35
Crossbill	*Loxia curvirostra*	36
Lesser Redpoll	*Acanthis cabaret*	36
Spotted Flycatcher	*Muscicapa striata*	37
Pied Flycatcher	*Ficedula hypoleuca*	37
Black Woodpecker	*Dryocopus martius*	38
Great Spotted Woodpecker	*Dendrocopos major*	38
Green Woodpecker	*Picus viridis*	39
Treecreeper	*Certhia familiaris*	39

SCIENTIFIC NAMES 123

Nuthatch	*Sitta europaea*	39
Jay	*Garrulus glandarius*	40
Hoopoe	*Upupa epops*	40
Cuckoo	*Cuculus canorus*	41
Tawny Owl	*Strix aluco*	41
Pheasant	*Phasianus colchicus*	44
Red-legged Partridge	*Alectoris rufa*	45
Grey Partridge	*Perdix perdix*	45
Red Grouse	*Lagopus lagopus scoticus*	45
Carrion Crow	*Corvus corone*	46
Rook	*Corvus frugilegus*	46
Hooded Crow	*Corvus cornix*	47
Jackdaw	*Corvus monedula*	47
Raven	*Corvus corax*	47
Meadow Pipit	*Anthus pratensis*	48
Tree Pipit	*Anthus trivialis*	48
Rock Pipit	*Anthus petrosus*	48
Skylark	*Alauda arvensis*	49
Crested Lark	*Galerida cristata*	49
Woodlark	*Lullula arborea*	49
Wheatear	*Oenanthe oenanthe*	50
Stonechat	*Saxicola torquata*	50
Whitethroat	*Sylvia communis*	51
Subalpine Warbler	*Sylvia cantillans*	51
Corn Bunting	*Emberiza calandra*	52
Yellowhammer	*Emberiza citrinella*	52
Reed Bunting	*Emberiza schoeniclus*	53, 88
Linnet	*Carduelis cannabina*	53
Kestrel	*Falco tinnunculus*	54
Sparrowhawk	*Accipiter nisus*	54
Hobby	*Falco subbuteo*	54
Peregrine	*Falco peregrinus*	55
Hen Harrier	*Circus cyaneus*	55
Marsh Harrier	*Circus aeruginosus*	57
Red Kite	*Milvus milvus*	56
Buzzard	*Buteo buteo*	56
Osprey	*Pandion haliaetus*	57
Mallard	*Anas platyrhynchos*	62, 64
Gadwall	*Anas strepera*	62, 64
Shoveler	*Anas clypeata*	62, 64
Wigeon	*Anas penelope*	63, 65
Teal	*Anas crecca*	63, 65
Pintail	*Anas acuta*	63, 65
Tufted Duck	*Aythya fuligula*	66, 68
Pochard	*Aythya ferina*	66, 68
Goldeneye	*Bucephala clangula*	66, 68
Goosander	*Mergus merganser*	67, 69
Red-breasted Merganser	*Mergus serrator*	67, 69
Eider	*Somateria mollissima*	67, 69
Great Crested Grebe	*Podiceps cristatus*	72
Little Grebe	*Tachybaptus ruficollis*	72
Shelduck	*Tadorna tadorna*	73
Coot	*Fulica atra*	73
Moorhen	*Gallinula chloropus*	73
Canada Goose	*Branta canadensis*	74
Greylag Goose	*Anser anser*	74

SCIENTIFIC NAMES

Common Name	Scientific Name	Page
Pink-footed Goose	*Anser brachyrhynchus*	75
Brent Goose	*Branta bernicla*	75
White-fronted Goose	*Anser albifrons*	75
Grey Heron	*Ardea cinerea*	76
Little Egret	*Egretta garzetta*	76
White Stork	*Ciconia ciconia*	76
Mute Swan	*Cygnus olor*	77
Whooper Swan	*Cygnus cygnus*	77
Bewick's Swan	*Cygnus columbianus*	77
Lapwing	*Vanellus vanellus*	78
Golden Plover	*Pluvialis apricaria*	78
Grey Plover	*Pluvialis squatarola*	79
Avocet	*Recurvirostra avosetta*	79
Green Sandpiper	*Tringa ochropus*	80
Common Sandpiper	*Actitis hypoleucos*	80
Snipe	*Gallinago gallinago*	80
Oystercatcher	*Haematopus ostralegus*	81
Greenshank	*Tringa nebularia*	81
Redshank	*Tringa totanus*	81
Curlew	*Numenius arquata*	82
Black-tailed Godwit	*Limosa limosa*	82
Bar-tailed Godwit	*Limosa lapponica*	82
Dunlin	*Calidris alpina*	83
Sanderling	*Calidris alba*	83
Knot	*Calidris canutus*	83
Turnstone	*Arenaria interpres*	84
Little Stint	*Callidris minuta*	84
Ringed Plover	*Charadrius hiaticula*	85
Little Ringed Plover	*Charadrius dubius*	85
Reed Warbler	*Acrocephalus scirpaceus*	86
Grasshopper Warbler	*Locustella naevia*	86
Sedge Warbler	*Acrocephalus schoenobaenus*	87
Cetti's Warbler	*Cettia cetti*	87
Kingfisher	*Alcedo atthis*	88
Pied Wagtail	*Motacilla alba*	89
Grey Wagtail	*Motacilla cinerea*	89
Yellow Wagtail	*Motacilla flava*	89
Herring Gull	*Larus argentatus*	92
Lesser Black-backed Gull	*Larus fuscus*	92
Great Black-backed Gull	*Larus marinus*	93
Yellow-legged Gull	*Larus michahellis*	93
Black-headed Gull	*Chroicocephalus ridibundus*	94
Common Gull	*Larus canus*	94
Mediterranean Gull	*Larus melanocephalus*	95
Kittiwake	*Rissa tridactyla*	95
Fulmar	*Fulmarus glacialis*	95
Common Tern	*Sterna hirundo*	98
Arctic Tern	*Sterna paradisaea*	98
Sandwich Tern	*Sterna sandvicensis*	99
Little Tern	*Sternula albifrons*	99
Puffin	*Fratercula arctica*	100
Guillemot	*Uria aalge*	100
Razorbill	*Alca torda*	101
Black Guillemot	*Cepphus grylle*	101
Gannet	*Morus bassanus*	102
Cormorant	*Phalacrocorax carbo*	102
Shag	*Phalacrocorax aristotelis*	102

Glossary

Birdwatching has its own jargon. You need to learn very little, and hardly any new words, but a few terms can help you to understand birds better and to describe them with greater precision.

Beak (or bill) Projecting jaws covered with a horny sheath.

Bird of prey A bird that preys on small birds or other animals.

Breeding plumage Plumage in which males display to females in order to mate – often called "summer plumage" but can occur during winter if that is when the birds pair up, as in the case of ducks.

Call (or call note) Short notes used by birds to keep in touch. Louder "flight calls" are helpful in identification, especially of wading birds.

Cap A patch of colour on top of the head.

Covert One of a patch or row of smaller feathers overlying the base of larger wing or tail feathers.

Drake A male duck. ("duck" is then used for the female, but is also used of the whole species in a more general sense.)

Eclipse Dull, female-like plumage of male ducks in summer.

Eye-ring A ring of colour, of either fleshy skin or feathers, around the eye.

Eye-stripe A line of colour through the eye, above the cheeks; a line above the eye is an "eyebrow" or, more correctly, a "superciliary stripe".

Habitat The type of environment a species lives in, providing food, resting sites, and, in summer, nest sites.

Immature A bird that is not yet fully sexually mature.

Juvenile A young bird in its first full covering of feathers.

Migration A regular movement of birds between different geographical areas inhabited at different times of year.

Moult The regular process of shedding and replacing feathers.

Moustache A stripe of colour from the bill, beneath the cheek.

Ornithology The scientific study of birds.

Passage migrant A bird that appears in a certain area only during spring or autumn migration.

Plumage The covering of feathers. Also various overall patterns or colours that identify different ages, sexes, and seasonal changes, such as adult winter or immature female.

Roost To roost (to sleep) or a roost (a place where birds spend the night, or non-feeding periods such as high tide).

Song A particular type of vocal performance that identifies a species, used mostly but not always by males to advertise their presence to others.

Species A "kind" of bird, individuals of which can interbreed and produce fertile, viable young; hybrids between species ("mules") are generally infertile.

Twitching Travelling to try to see a particular bird of a rare species (often a "vagrant", far from its usual range) – not the same as "birdwatching".

Wader A shoreline bird: a plover, sandpiper, or allied species.

Index

Page numbers in **bold** indicate main entry.

A B

Arctic Tern **98**, 107
Avocet **79**, 109, 120
Bar-tailed Godwit **82**, 121
behaviour 13
Bewick's Swan **77**, 105
birds of prey 58
bird song 11
Black Guillemot **101**, 109
Black Woodpecker **38**, 111
Black-headed Gull **94**, 105, 106
Black-tailed Godwit **82**, 121
Blackbird **23** (female), **24** (male), 108, 112
Blackcap **34**, 111
Blue Tit **26**, 116, 118
Brambling **21**, 114
Brent Goose **75**, 108
Bullfinch **21**, 105, 115
Bunting
  Corn **52**, 113
  Reed **53** (male), **88** (female), 113
Buzzard **56**, 115

C

Canada Goose **74**, 108, 114
Carrion Crow **46**, 110
Cetti's Warbler **87**, 111
Chaffinch **21**, 114
Chiffchaff **34**, 117
Coal Tit **27**, 106
Collared Dove **29**, 105
colour and markings 9
Common Gull **94**, 106
Common Sandpiper **80**, 121
Common Tern **98**, 107
Coot **73**, 108, 111
Cormorant **102**, 110
Corn Bunting **52**, 113
Crested Lark **49**, 112
Crossbill **36**, 116, 119
Crow
  Carrion **46**, 110
  Hooded **47**, 105
Cuckoo **41**, 105
Curlew **82**, 120

DEF

Dove
  Collared **29**, 105
  Stock **29**, 104
  Turtle **29**, 113, 117
Duck, Tufted **66** (male), **68** (female), 109, 111
ducks 70
Dunlin **83**, 121
Dunnock **18**, 111
Egret, Little **76**, 105, 109
Eider **67** (male), **69** (female), 109, 114
Fieldfare **23**, 113
flight pattern 11
Flycatcher
  Pied **37**, 107, 110
  Spotted **37**, 111
Fulmar **95**, 107

G

Gadwall **62** (male), **64** (female), 104, 112
Gannet **102**, 108
Godwit
  Bar-tailed **82**, 121
  Black-tailed **82**, 121
Goldcrest **35**, 116, 119
Golden Plover **78**, 120
Goldeneye **66** (male), **68** (female), 104, 108
Goldfinch **20**, 118
Goosander **67** (male), **69** (female), 104, 109, 117
Goose
  Brent **75**, 108
  Canada **74**, 108, 114
  Greylag **74**, 115
  Pink-footed **75**, 115
  White-fronted **75**, 115
Grasshopper Warbler **86**, 112
Great Black-backed Gull **93**, 108
Great Crested Grebe **72**, 117
Great Spotted Woodpecker **38**, 108
Great Tit **26**, 116, 118
Grebe
  Great Crested **72**, 117
  Little **72**, 110, 117
Green Sandpiper **80**, 121
Green Woodpecker **39**, 117
Greenfinch **20**, 116, 119
Greenshank **81**, 120, 121
Grey Heron **76**, 105
Grey Partridge **45**, 114
Grey Plover **79**, 121
Grey Wagtail **89**, 104, 119
Greylag Goose **74**, 115
Grouse, Red **45**, 115, 116
Guillemot **100**, 108
Guillemot, Black **101**, 109
Gull
  Black-headed **94**, 105, 106
  Common **94**, 106
  Great Black-backed **93**, 108
  Herring **92**, 105, 107
  Lesser Black-backed **92**, 107, 109
  Mediterranean **95**, 106
  Yellow-legged **93**, 106
gulls 96

HIJK

Harrier
  Hen **55**, 104, 115
  Marsh **57**, 111, 114
Hen Harrier **55**, 104, 116
Heron, Grey **76**, 105
Herring Gull **92**, 105, 107
Hobby **54**, 107
Hooded Crow **47**, 105
Hoopoe **40**, 109, 116
House Martin **30**, 107, 119
House Sparrow **18**, 111, 112
identifying birds 8–14
Jackdaw **47**, 109
Jay **40**, 110, 118
Kestrel **54**, 115
Kingfisher **88**, 117, 118
Kite, Red **56**, 114, 119
Kittiwake **95**, 106, 107
Knot **83**, 120

LM

Lapwing **78**, 109, 116, 121
Lark, Crested **49**, 112
Lesser Black-backed Gull **92**, 107, 109
Lesser Redpoll **36**, 113, 116
Linnet **53**, 112, 115
Little Egret **76**, 105, 109
Little Grebe **72**, 110, 117
Little Ringed Plover **85**, 121
Little Stint **84**, 120
Little Tern **99**, 106
Long-tailed Tit **27**, 106
Magpie **25**, 108
Mallard **62** (male), **64** (female), 104, 112, 117, 119
Marsh Harrier **57**, 111, 114
Marsh Tit **27**, 110

INDEX

Martin
  House **30**, 107, 119
  Sand **31**, 111
Meadow Pipit **48**, 113
Mediterranean Gull **95**, 106
Merganser, Red-breasted, **67** (male), **69** (female), 104, 106
Mistle Thrush **22**, 112
Moorhen **73**, 109, 119
Mute Swan **77**, 104

N O P

Nightingale **35**, 110, 118
Nuthatch **39**, 105, 117
Osprey **57**, 114
Owl, Tawny **41**, 114
Oystercatcher **81**, 120
Partridge
  Grey **45**, 114
  Red-legged **45**, 114
Peregrine **55**, 106
Pheasant **44**, 114, 115, 117
Pied Flycatcher **37**, 107, 110
Pied Wagtail **89**, 106
Pigeon, Town **28**, 104
Pink-footed Goose **75**, 115
Pintail **63** (male), **65** (female), 105, 113
Pipit
  Meadow **48**, 113
  Rock **48**, 113
  Tree **48**, 113
Plover
  Golden **78**, 120
  Grey **79**, 121
  Little Ringed **85**, 121
  Ringed **85**, 120, 121
Pochard **66** (male), **68** (female), 105, 114, 116
Puffin **100**, 108

R S

Raven **47**, 110
Razorbill **101**, 108
Red Grouse **45**, 115, 116
Red Kite **56**, 114, 119
Red-breasted Merganser **67** (male), **69** (female), 104, 106
Red-legged Partridge **45**, 114
Redpoll, Lesser **36**, 113, 116
Redshank **81**, 120
Redstart **35**, 115, 118
Redwing **23**, 113, 115
Reed Bunting **53** (male), **88** (female), 113
Reed Warbler **86**, 110
Ringed Plover **85**, 120, 121
Robin **19**, 115
Rock Pipit **48**, 113
Rook **46**, 109
Sand Martin **31**, 111
Sanderling **83**, 120
Sandpiper
  Common **80**, 121
  Green **80**, 121
Sandwich Tern **99**, 107
scientific names 122
season 12
Sedge Warbler **87**, 112
Shag **102**, 111
shape of bird 9
Shelduck **73**, 109
Shoveler **62** (male), **64** (female), 112, 117
Siskin **20**, 117, 118
size of bird 8
Skylark **49**, 112
Snipe **80**, 120
Song Thrush **22**, 112
sound 11
Sparrow
  House **18**, 111, 112
  Tree **19**, 112
Sparrowhawk **54**, 115
Spotted Flycatcher **37**, 111
Starling **24**, 108, 116
Stint, Little **84**, 120
Stock Dove **29**, 104
Stonechat **50**, 107, 113, 115
Stork, White, **76**, 105, 109
Subalpine Warbler **51**, 114
Swallow **30**, 118
Swan
  Bewick's **77**, 105
  Mute **77**, 104
  Whooper **77**, 104
Swift **31**, 110

T

tail shape 10
Tawny Owl **41**, 114
Teal **63** (male), **65** (female), 105, 113, 117
Tern
  Arctic **98**, 107
  Common **98**, 107
  Little **99**, 106
  Sandwich **99**, 107
Thrush
  Mistle **22**, 112
  Song **22**, 112
Tit
  Blue **26**, 116, 118
  Coal **27**, 106
  Great **26**, 116, 118
  Long-tailed **27**, 106
  Marsh **27**, 110
Town Pigeon **28**, 104
Tree Pipit **48**, 113
Tree Sparrow, **19**, 112
Treecreeper **39**, 110
Tufted Duck **66** (male), **68** (female), 109, 111
Turnstone **84**, 120
Turtle Dove **29**, 113, 117

W Y

Wagtail
  Grey **89**, 104, 119
  Pied **89**, 106
  Yellow **89**, 116, 119
Warbler
  Cetti's **87**, 111
  Grasshopper **86**, 112
  Reed **86**, 110
  Sedge **87**, 112
  Subalpine **51**, 114
  Willow **34**, 117, 119
Waxwing **25**, 111, 117
Wheatear **50**, 104
White Stork **76**, 105, 109
White-fronted Goose **75**, 115
Whitethroat **51**, 111
Whooper Swan **77**, 104
Wigeon **63** (male), **65** (female), 105, 113, 116
Willow Warbler **34**, 117, 119
wing shape 10
Woodlark **49**, 113
Woodpecker
  Black **38**, 111
  Great Spotted **38**, 108
  Green **39**, 117
Woodpigeon **28**, 104
Wren **19**, 110
Yellow Wagtail **89**, 116, 119
Yellow-legged Gull **93**, 106
Yellowhammer **52**, 112, 118, 119

Acknowledgments

Dorling Kindersley would like to thank: RSPB consultant Mark Boyd; David Roberts for database support; Claire Bowers and Susie Peachey, DK Picture Library; Jamie Ambrose for editorial; Ann Kay for proofreading; Vritti Bansal for design; Oliver Metcalf for content suggestions; and Suhita Dharamjit, Senior Jackets Designer. The publisher would also like to thank the following for their kind permission to reproduce their photographs: (**Key**: a-above; b-below/bottom; c-centre; f-far; l-left; r-right; t-top)

4 Alamy Images: Arco Images GmbH (br). **6-7 Getty Images / iStock:** BirdImages (cra); Neil Bowman (cl). **9 Robert Royse:** (tl). **Dreamstime.com:** Mikalay Varabey (cra). **11 Getty Images / iStock:** Neil Bowman (cr). **12 Dreamstime.com:** Ornitolog (crb). **Shutterstock.com:** rubacolor (b). **13 Getty Images / iStock:** unpict (cla). **14 FLPA:** Franz Christoph Robi / Imagebroker (bc). **15 Corbis:** Glenn Bartley / All Canada Photos. **16-17 Corbis:** Paul Thompson. **17 Dreamstime.com:** Dennis Jacobsen (tr). **18 123RF.com:** pegleg01 (b). **22 Dreamstime.com:** Sandra Standbridge (t). **23 123RF.com:** dpotashkin (c). **26 Getty Images / iStock:** unpict (t). **29 Christopher Taylor:** (tc). **Getty Images / iStock:** Andrew_Howe (c). **30 Dreamstime.com:** Dennis Jacobsen (b); Mikalay Varabey (t). **31 Dreamstime.com:** Anthony Baggett (t). **36 Dreamstime.com:** Mikelane45 (t). **41 Getty Images / iStock:** Peter Clayton Wildlife Photography (t). **48 Dreamstime.com:** Ornitolog (c). **51 Dreamstime.com:** Tatyana Zarubo (t). **54 Robert Royse:** (bc). **59 Dreamstime.com:** Chris Lorenz (t). **60 Getty Images / iStock:** PrinPrince (br). **61 Getty Images / iStock:** Andyworks (bl). **62-63 naturepl.com:** Peter Cairns. **62 Robert Royse:** (br). **63 Getty Images / iStock:** BirdImages (b). **66 Markus Varesvuo:** (c). **67 Melvin Grey:** (bc). **68 Alamy Stock Photo:** imageBROKER / Stefan Huwiler (c). **69 Robert Royse:** (bc). **Getty Images:** Corbis / Hal Beral (c). **70 Markus Varesvuo:** (ca). **71 Melvin Grey:** (c). **Robert Royse:** (bc, br). **73 Robert Royse:** (br). **76 Robert Royse:** (bc). **79 Dreamstime.com:** Maria Itina (b). **80 Robert Royse:** (bc). **81 Getty Images / iStock:** Neil Bowman (b). **83 Getty Images / iStock:** BirdImages (b). **85 Alamy Images:** Simon Stirrup (bl). **86 Alamy Stock Photo:** Alan Williams (b). **Getty Images / iStock:** Andyworks (t). **87 Robert Royse:** (bc). **Alamy images:** Alan Williams (bl). **88 Getty Images / iStock:** PrinPrince (t). **90-91 Getty Images:** Anthony Thomas. **90 Getty Images / iStock:** Neil Bowman (br). **91 Robert Royse:** (tl). **96 Richard Ford / digitalwildlife.co.uk:** (bc). **99 Getty Images / iStock:** Wirestock (t). **101 Robert Royse:** (bc). **103 Alamy Images:** Arco Images GmbH (bn). **104 Dorling Kindersley:** Neil Fletcher; Roger Tidman; Mark Hamblin; George McCarthy; Markus Varesvuo; Melvin Grey; Mike Lane; Chris Gomersall Photography; Philip Newman. **Getty Images:** Corbis / Hal Beral (crb). **105 Dorling Kindersley:** David Cottridge; David Tipling; Roger Tidman; Mark Hamblin; Chris Gomersall Photography; Roger Wilmshurst. **Getty Images / iStock:** BirdImages; Andrew_Howe; Peter Clayton Wildlife Photography. **106 Dorling Kindersley:** Hanne Eriksen / Jens Eriksen; Mike Lane; Steve Young; Roger Tidman; Chris Gomersall Photography; Roger Wilmshurst; Melvin Grey. **E. J. Peiker. 107 Dorling Kindersley:** Chris Gomersall Photography; Roger Wilmshurst; Mike Lane; Mark Hamblin. **Dreamstime.com:** Dennis Jacobsen (bc). **Getty Images / iStock:** Wirestock (cra). **E. J. Peiker. Roger Wilmshurst. 108 Chris Gomersall Photography. David Tipling Photo Library. Dorling Kindersley:** Neil Fletcher; Chris Gomersall Photography; Roger Tidman; Frank Greenaway / Arundel Wildfowl Trust, West Sussex; Mark Hamblin. **109 Chris Gomersall Photography. Dorling Kindersley:** David Cottridge; Chris Gomersall Photography; Neil Fletcher; Mike Lane; George McCarthy; Roger Tidman; Steve Young; Jari Peltomaki; Roger Wilmshurst. **Dreamstime.com:** Maria Itina (tr). **110 Dorling Kindersley:** Hanne Eriksen / Jens Eriksen; Chris Gomersall Photography; Mike Lane; Mark Hamblin; Roger Tidman; Steve Young. **Getty Images / iStock:** Andyworks (cr). **David Cottridge; Mike Lane; Mark Hamblin; Chris Gomersall Photography; Tomi Muukkonen; Markus Varesvuo. **Dreamstime.com:** Anthony Baggett (ca); Tatyana Zarubo (c). **112 123RF.com:** pegleg01 (tc). **Alamy Stock Photo:** Alan Williams (r). **Dorling Kindersley:** Greg Dean / Yvonne Dean; Mike Lane; Hanne Eriksen / Jens Eriksen; Chris Gomersall Photography; Chris Gomersall; Roger Tidman; Melvin Grey; Markus Varesvuo. **Dreamstime.com:** Sandra Standbridge (cb). **113 123RF.com:** dpotashkin (cb). **Dorling Kindersley:** Hanne Eriksen / Jens Eriksen; Markus Varesvuo; Roger Wilmshurst; Mark Hamblin; Mike Lane; Roger Tidman; David Tipling; Steve Young; Melvin Grey. **Dreamstime.com:** Mikelane45 (cl); Ornitolog (tc). **114 Alamy Stock Photo:** imageBROKER / Stefan Huwiler (b). **Dorling Kindersley:** Greg Dean / Yvonne Dean; George McCarthy; Chris Gomersall Photography; Melvin Grey; Mark Hamblin; Neil Fletcher; Mike Lane; Roger Tidman. **115 Dorling Kindersley:** Greg Dean / Yvonne Dean; Arie Ouwerkerk; George McCarthy; Hanne Eriksen / Jens Eriksen; Mike Lane; David Tipling; Chris Gomersall Photography; Roger Wilmshurst; Mark Hamblin. **116 Dorling Kindersley:** Hanne Eriksen / Jens Eriksen; Markus Varesvuo; Chris Gomersall Photography; Roger Wilmshurst; Melvin Grey; Mark Hamblin; Neil Fletcher. **Dreamstime.com:** Mikelane45 (tc). **Getty Images / iStock:** unpict (crb). **117 Dorling Kindersley:** Chris Gomersall Photography; Mike Lane; David Tipling; Mark Hamblin; Roger Tidman. **Getty Images / iStock:** PrinPrince (tc). **118 Dorling Kindersley:** David Cottridge ; Mark Hamblin; Roger Wilmshurst; David Tipling; Chris Gomersall. **Dreamstime.com:** Mikalay Varabey (b). **Getty Images / iStock:** PrinPrince (tr); unpict (br). **119 Dorling Kindersley:** Chris Gomersall; George McCarthy; Melvin Grey; Markus Varesvuo; Mark Hamblin. **Dreamstime.com:** Dennis Jacobsen (tl). **120 Alamy Stock Photo:** Simon Stirrup (cl). **Dorling Kindersley:** Chris Gomersall Photography; Markus Varesvuo; Roger Tidman; Mike Lane; George McCarthy; Steve Young; Chris Gomersall. **Dreamstime.com:** Maria Itina (br). **Getty Images / iStock:** Neil Bowman (c). **121 Dorling Kindersley:** David Cottridge; Chris Gomersall; Markus Varesvuo; George McCarthy; Mike Lane; Neil Fletcher. **Getty Images / iStock:** BirdImages (tr)

Cover images: *Front:* **Alamy Stock Photo:** Colin Varndell l; **Chris Gomersall Photography:** cra; **Dorling Kindersley:** Roger Wilmshurst cr; **rspb-images.com:** Mark Hamblin crb; *Back:* **Dreamstime.com:** Assoonas tl; **Getty Images:** Bryan Mullennix / Stone cl; **rspb-images.com:** Nigel Blake clb; *Spine:* **Alamy Stock Photo:** Colin Varndell

The RSPB is the UK's largest nature conservation charity, working locally in the UK, and around the world. Our vision is a shared world where wildlife, wild places and all people thrive. We act by protecting and restoring habitats, saving species and helping to end the nature and climate emergency. Nature is in crisis. Together we can save it.

To find out more about the RSPB and how to become a member visit **rspb.org.uk**

Dorling Kindersley will donate a minimum of 2% of sales income received for this book to RSPB Sales Ltd, the trading subsidiary of RSPB (registered charity in England and Wales no 207076 and in Scotland no SC037654)

Other books published by DK with the RSPB include:
RSPB Pocket Birds of Britain and Europe
RSPB Birds of Britain and Europe
RSPB Complete Birds of Britain and Europe